Writing for College

Writing for College
A No-B.S. Guide

ROBERT ALDEN RUBIN

McFarland & Company, Inc., Publishers
Jefferson, North Carolina

ISBN (print) 978-1-4766-7366-0
ISBN (ebook) 978-1-4766-3249-0

LIBRARY OF CONGRESS CATALOGUING DATA ARE AVAILABLE

BRITISH LIBRARY CATALOGUING DATA ARE AVAILABLE

© 2018 Robert Alden Rubin. All rights reserved

No part of this book may be reproduced or transmitted in any form or by any means, electronic or mechanical, including photocopying or recording, or by any information storage and retrieval system, without permission in writing from the publisher.

Front cover image of student with writer's block © 2018 Aleutie/iStock

Printed in the United States of America

*McFarland & Company, Inc., Publishers
Box 611, Jefferson, North Carolina 28640
www.mcfarlandpub.com*

For Raoul
(Tag! Got you last)

Acknowledgments

The poem "Good Morning, Love," by Paul Blackburn, appears courtesy of Joan Blackburn, Copyright © 1985 by Joan Blackburn.

Thanks to Walter Beale for permission to adapt and excerpt material from *Real Writing: Argumentation, Reflection, Information*, Copyright © 1986 by Walter H. Beale.

My gratitude to Professor Laura Fine of Meredith College for reviewing and commenting on the manuscript, and to Jake Vaccaro, of Meredith's Carlyle Campbell Library, for offering suggestions about working with librarians.

Table of Contents

Acknowledgments   vi
Introduction: Be Interesting, or "B.S."?   1

I: Style and the Academy

1. Who's Listening?   4
2. Blinded by Science   10
3. Subject and Object   17
4. Data   22
5. Specific Versus General   26
6. Active Voice, Active Mind   33
7. Rhythm and Emphasis   37

II: Argument and Persuasion

8. A Jury of Your Peers   44
9. Who Says? And So What?   51
10. Claim, Warrant and Support   57
11. Writing the Analytical Paragraph   61
12. Classical Argumentation   64
13. "B.S." and How to Detect It   67

III: Research and Preparation

14. Writing for Yourself   74
15. The eScholar and the Library   82
16. Quotation and Documentation   88
17. The Critical Lens   96

Table of Content

IV: Writing the College Essay

18. The Open House	100
19. Introduction and Threshold	105
20. Agent and Thesis	112
21. Plan	119
22. Conclusion and Takeaway	138
23. A Short Chapter on Titles	145
24. Revision: The Second Look	150
Appendix 1. Logical Fallacies	155
Appendix 2. Style Guides	161
Appendix 3. Writing in the Sciences	170
Index	179

Introduction:
Be Interesting, or "B.S."?

An academic dialect is perfected when its terms are hard to understand and refer only to one another. —Mason Cooley

Reading requires effort these days. In a culture where attention deficit isn't so much a disorder as a way of life, where cascading images and loud messages constantly yammer for you to respond, reading requires focus and reflection.

So, when you write, have pity on your reader. Make it interesting!

"Even academic writing?" you ask. Absolutely. College writers tackle complicated ideas that usually get ignored by popular culture, but that doesn't mean they have to be boring. You'll read plenty of hard stuff in the library stacks and online databases before you finish college—why compound the problem by writing blandly about it?

That's this guide's stand, at least. Here you'll find a skeptical, prescriptive look at how to write in college—rules and suggestions that apply whether you're writing for Econ or English, or just for yourself. It favors clear, active prose, careful thinking, lively specifics, and thoughtful organization. Once you master those fundamentals, you can adapt them to specific demands of format and structure that may govern your particular academic specialty.

Don't make the mistake of thinking you're just writing for your professor. What you learn in college writing classes will stay with you for the rest of your life. Maybe your professor is the only one who will see your writing now, but pretty soon you'll be out of college and writing for real. Why not start doing it well? (Your professor will certainly appreciate it!)

So, you ask, what makes some writing good and some bad?

Some of today's writing teachers argue that we've witnessed a steady shift away from "privileged" standards of prose that society once held up as ideals—that there's no "bad" writing, only "ineffective" writing.

Introduction

No such thing as bad writing? That's like saying there are no bad baseball players, only ineffective ones. It sounds kind of like "B.S.," don't you think?

Is it only coincidence that as these attitudes have flourished, more and more dull, jargon-heavy sludge has been extruded from the gates of academe?

Don't add to the pile. Whether you seek the Bachelor of Arts (B.A.), the Bachelor of Sciences (B.S.), or another degree, there's no justifying B.S. You can do better. Writing interesting, literate English prose offers many rewards, not least of which is the attention of readers who will take your ideas seriously.

This book will show you how to get it.

I: Style and the Academy

*Or, Why Sounding "Academic"
Isn't the Same as Being an Academic*

1

Who's Listening?

Skepticism, like chastity, should not be relinquished too readily.—George Santayana

So, you're a skeptic about college writing, are you? "The only reason I have to write papers is that my professor is making me," you say. "It's not like anyone else will ever read them. Why should I have to worry about style, or structure, or MLA or APA formats—or footnotes, for godsake? Can't I just go to lectures and study for exams?"

It's a reasonable question. The short answer is, "No." That's not the way it works. College professors have found that writing papers helps you learn to think critically. They want you to go through the discipline of learning to do it as a way of training your mind. But even if that weren't true, even if you were out there in the "real world" where no one asks for footnoted papers, it's worth considering the question that it brings up: Who[1] are you really writing for?

The answer: it depends. Sometimes you write for yourself, writing to learn. Sometimes you write for others, writing to communicate. Usually it's a little of both. Here's how they're different:

Writing for Yourself—You take notes, write journals, compose drafts, and brainstorm on paper to help you understand, remember, or explore a subject.

Writing for Others—You write and edit letters, reports, essays, memos, fiction, or poems to convey information or ideas to a reader.

Both of these ways of writing are part of the same process of thinking and learning, and they aren't mutually exclusive. Let's consider them in more detail.

---

1. Or, as your author might say if he were writing for a grammarian instead of you, "For whom are you really writing?"

1. Who's Listening?

Writing for Yourself

Have you ever found yourself reading a book or listening to a lecture and realized you've forgotten everything from the last ten minutes? Time to get out the index cards, notebook, smartphone, or laptop computer and start writing things down!

When you write for yourself, you're mostly writing to learn. Taking notes and summarizing readings forces you to translate ideas into language; as a result, you have to think about them. Of course, you'll need the notes when it comes time to study for exams, but note-taking does more than that. It helps move material out of your short-term memory, from which it will quickly fade, and into your long-term memory, where you can find it when you need to. Even if the ideas you jot down don't stick at first, notes can help you reconstruct them later on. Seeing a particular word or sequence of ideas in your notes may loosen a thread that leads into the depths of your memory, out of which you can fish the original idea and bring it flip-flopping back into the boat.

Even with more formal writing, such as a term paper or a lab report for class, in some sense you're still writing for yourself. Composing a sentence, a paragraph, or an essay forces you to slow down, think about what you're saying, and examine what you've learned. Your professors want you to go through the discipline of considering a topic, reviewing data critically, and trying to organize your thoughts into a coherent argument, and they believe that writing will encourage you to do it.

In the process, they figure, you might just discover something.

Writing for Others

When you write for others, you're writing to communicate. "Duh," you say. But—*duh!*—a lot of writers just don't get that. They expect their audience to read their minds, rather than their words.

At its most basic level, communication means moving ideas and information from your head to somebody else's. Since your reader can't, in fact, read your mind, you give him your thoughts using the symbols and syntax that we call language.

Unfortunately, between your head and your reader's head lies what computer engineers might call a "bandwidth problem." Your brain has to code your knowledge into language, then transmit an analog signal (spoken, written, or gestured) by way of your sensory inputs and outputs (eyes, ears, hands, and mouth). Your reader must do the same thing, in reverse. All that coding, transmission, and decoding takes time.

However you communicate, a lot gets lost in translation—you only have time to convey a little of what you know and think, and must choose carefully because your reader can't spend forever figuring out every nuance of your intended message. Fortunately, with writing, once you've put the words down on paper, they stop being transient thoughts and become permanent "things" that you can manipulate. You can refine them so that you pack a lot of information into a few well chosen words. That's why, if you're a good writer, you don't just turn in your first draft. You review and revise it, typically in three ways:

Ruminating—Looking critically at the information you intend to transmit, turning it over and over again to make sure you've made your key points.
Empathizing—Putting yourself in the reader's shoes, and imagining reading what you've just written.
Comparing—Evaluating what you want to say with what you think the reader will hear, and deciding whether your meaning comes across.

Don't worry about making it perfect the first time. If you want to become a better writer, give yourself permission to explore your topic as you rewrite! Whether you're writing for yourself or for others, remember that it's a *way of thinking*, of using language to capture and examine what you know or what you've learned. A college paper presents those thoughts in an organized way, and tries to make a point. That means at some point you have to put your words to the test: will someone find it interesting? Writing for others, whether it be your professors, your classmates, or for publication, requires you to learn your subject well enough to tell others about it coherently, and interest them enough that they'll follow your thoughts. By doing so, you bring ideas to life, which is part of the purpose of college in the first place.

So, what do your college professors expect? While it may sometimes seem as if they expect you to jump through arbitrary academic hoops, what they're really hoping for is *intelligent discourse*.

Intelligent Discourse

Your professors don't want to hear from bots that spew out contextless facts and prefabricated academic phrases: they can use Google too. Rather,

1. Who's Listening?

they want to know *you*, and to know what your reasoned opinions are. They call it "critical thinking," and it's the most important thing you can learn at college. Your professors are more interested in that than in how "academic" you sound.

Many of the rules you were taught in high school are just shortcuts to help you sound intelligent. Don't get too hung up on them. For example, can you use the first person ("I") in a college essay? Sure,[2] if you're discussing your conclusions about the evidence. How about colloquial English? Yes, in the right situation. Sentence fragments? If used deliberately, and for effect (like the one in the previous sentence), why not?

Again, it's a question of audience. Who are you writing for? When you take notes, you're writing only for yourself. When you write an article for an academic journal, you're writing for experts. Obviously, you don't write the same way for both audiences.

In this guide, for instance, your author (me) speaks directly to you, making ironic comments to keep you interested and even using a few ungrammatical sentence fragments for effect—to sound informal and clever. That's appropriate for a practical handbook aimed at skeptical students. If I'd written a theoretical treatise on English composition for an academic audience, though, I'd change my tone.

A good rule of thumb: the more "scientific" the subject matter, or the more scholarly the audience, the more formal your language should be. Most college papers don't have to be written as if they're being submitted to a formal, peer-reviewed scholarly journal, but they shouldn't be, like, slang. They should be the sort of intelligent discourse that sounds the way you would wish to sound if you were conversing with your professors in front of the rest of the class—if you only had the time to look up all your facts and prepare your arguments beforehand.

The nice thing about writing is that *you do*.

You don't have to turn into a faceless "anonymous student" when you write your college papers. You should sound like yourself, but *the best possible version of yourself*—a person with reasoned opinions based on carefully considered evidence. In college, where you're expected to know more than you

---

2. Why did your high school teachers say never to use the first person? Simple. Because most high school students, given the chance, will talk and talk about themselves, their opinions, and their feelings, and never stop. Teachers want to hear about what students know, not what they feel. And, as the saying goes, opinions are like … well … bellybuttons—everybody has one. So, what makes your opinions worth considering?

I: Style and the Academy

knew in high school, standards for content are higher, but the rules on style can actually be more flexible—once you know what they are.

Good writers learn the rules. Then they learn when and how to break them.

No "B.S." About

Audience

1. Know whom you're writing for.

The way you write depends on who's going to read it. If you're writing a text to friends, for instance, you don't need footnotes or formal salutations and complimentary closings. (In fact, your friends may think you're B.S.-ing them if you send a text or email that sounds like a job-application letter.) On the other hand, if you *are* writing a job-application letter, you won't get hired if you ignore conventions of punctuation, spelling, and formal correspondence, and address the Vice President for Hiring as, "Dude."

In college, most of your professors will require you to write papers as if they might someday be published. That doesn't mean you need to suck all the life out of your prose, but it does typically require certain formalities and a certain attitude toward the truth. This book explores both.

2. Put yourself in the reader's shoes.

If you were the reader, what would you want—or need—to know? Ask yourself that question, and be sure to get the answer into your writing. Often, in college papers, what the reader (your professor) most wants to know from you is, *"How do you know that?"* and, *"So what?"* Good college papers spend a lot of time exploring the question of where facts, opinions, and information come from, and why they're interesting. Prove your case!

3. Be honest.

If you're not an expert, don't fake it. If you're confused, examine what confuses you and discuss it—don't cover it up. If you're passionately convinced, make your case, with good reasons and data to support it. But sound like *you*. Your college professors don't want to hear students who write like clones of some anonymous "typical" student, they want to hear from *you*.

4. Don't just sound off.

Sounding like yourself is fine, but remember that your professor really

1. Who's Listening?

wants to see what you know and how you reason, not uninformed opinions. Before you begin filling your papers with "I feel" and "I think," keep in mind that the true art of good academic writing is making it sound as if it's based on reasoning and evidence, not gut reactions. After all, most of what you'll write about at college is ... *science*.

2

Blinded by Science

Art is science made clear.—Wilson Mizner

"Science?"

Why, you ask, should a book about college writing mention science? It's simple, really. College is all about science.

Most American universities have a "College of Arts and Sciences" where undergraduates start their college careers, and which administrators distinguish from more specialized professional schools of law, business, medicine, social work, and so forth. Curiously enough, despite its widespread currency, you won't find the term "Arts and Sciences" defined in most dictionaries or encyclopedias—not even in a massive scholarly tome such as the *Oxford English Dictionary*.

To understand the phrase, let's look at the academic departments in one school's "College of Arts and Sciences":

Africana Studies
American Studies
Anthropology
Art
Art Therapy
Biochemistry and Molecular Biology
Bioinformatics
Biological Sciences
Biomedical Sciences
Biostatistics and Epidemiology
Chemistry
Classical and Semitic Languages and Literatures
Communication
Counseling
Criminal Justice

Dramatic Literature
Early Modern European Studies
East Asian Languages and Literatures
Economics
Electronic Media
English
English as a Foreign Language
Environmental and Resource Policy
Epidemiology
Film Studies
Forensic Sciences
Genetics
Geography
German and Slavic Languages and Literatures

2. Blinded by Science

Historic Preservation	Pharmacology
History	Philosophy
Hominid Paleobiology	Physics
Human Sciences	Political Communication
Human Services	Political Management
Humanities	Political Science
Immunology	Professional Psychology
Journalism	Psychology
Judaic Studies	Public Policy and Public Administration
Legislative Affairs	
Linguistics	Religion
Mathematics	Romance Languages & Literatures
Media and Public Affairs	Sociology
Microbiology and Tropical Medicine	Speech and Hearing Science
	Statistics
Molecular and Cellular Oncology	Telecommunication
Museum Studies	Theatre & Dance
Music	University Writing
Neuroscience	Women and Leadership Programs
Organizational Sciences	Women's Studies
Peace Studies	

As you can see, at this university the college's departments range from hard sciences (such as physics) to fine arts (such as music). Historically, in the arts and sciences curriculum, science meant *knowing* and art meant *doing*, and college taught both the wisdom of the ages and the techniques of putting that wisdom to use.

These days, most of us have forgotten that (or never learned it in the first place). "Science" now connotes practical, empirical knowledge that we can test and verify. "Art" connotes airy aesthetic things that depend on taste. Both connotations mislead a lot of people.

Working out the mathematical implications of the theory of quantum mechanics may be science, but applying it as part of a computer model to predict global weather patterns is an art. Learning linguistic theory and cognitive psychology means learning science. Using that to usefully interpret Shakespeare's word choices or decode Chinese dialects requires art. In the academy, to practice most sciences requires art, just as practicing most arts—even "fine arts" like music and painting—requires knowing scientific principles such as harmonics and color theory.

And writing? Writing—even writing about the hardest of hard science—is most definitely an art.

I: Style and the Academy

Good Art

"An art?" you ask. "Even book reports and essay exams? Even case studies and class notes? Aren't there objective, empirical standards for what's good and what's not? What about all the picky rules of grammar, style, and usage that I can never keep straight? Why can't there be a simple, logical formula to learn?" The answer, simply put, is that arts such as writing are about *doing*, not about *knowing*.

You learn to write well by writing a lot, and by reading other writers. It's as simple—and as complicated—as that. It's more than memorizing rules of grammar. Unlike a computer running BASIC, or C++, or LISP, with exactly defined rules of syntax for the code, your readers won't crash if they encounter an English sentence full of errors. They may get disgusted and irritated, but they'll probably understand you if they work hard enough. They'll only do that work, though, if they have a compelling reason to. That's where the art of good writing comes in.

Bad Manners

Rules of writing come from convention and etiquette, not symbolic logic. Bad writing is, quite simply, *bad manners*.

What does that mean? It means that you don't dangle a participle for the same reason you don't wear cut-off jeans and a tank top to a formal dress party: because people will notice and make snide comments. Similarly, a garbled sentence is a discourtesy to a busy reader who doesn't have time to puzzle it out.

Compare it to the way you dress. No simple formula teaches you to dress fashionably or succeed socially; you just learn what people expect, and how to meet—or challenge—those expectations. Writing's essentially the same. While writing certainly builds on foundations of all sorts of sciences, such as linguistics, logic, psychology, and aesthetics, it takes its final shape from the social conventions that people use to live with each other. The art is in the mix. And *art* is the operative word.

Many excellent writers feel vaguely guilty that they can't diagram the grammar of an English sentence. Identifying misplaced modifiers and dangling participles; distinguishing between passive, expletive, and copular constructions (whatever those are); knowing whether clauses are restrictive or nonrestrictive—yikes! Most of us never master the grammar book that teaches those "rules," even though we know how to speak grammatical English. No wonder, then, that so many of us long for a nice, neat, model that strips all the art and

2. Blinded by Science

subjectivity out of writing and leaves just the facts, ma'am. No wonder that we try to write like scientists.

And no wonder that we're puzzled when people tell us they have trouble reading what we've written.

Fake Science

Somewhere between our wish for simple rules, and our misconception about what it means to be scientific, twenty-first century college prose got bogged down. It took on a faceless way of communicating that emphasized *things known* instead of *knowing things*. It tried to present the world as lists of stuff, untouched by human hands. Intending to write like scientists, many of us have ended up writing like bean-counters.

UCLA rhetorician Richard Lanham calls this way of writing the "Official Style," emphasizing *official* rather than *style*. He doesn't mean it as a compliment, either; it's the native language of bureaucrats, he suggests. Rather than reflecting expert use of precise terminology and empirical data, Lanham contends, the Official Style usually fakes expertise, as in this example from a freshman research paper:

> This formation of one-dimensional flows seems to apply exclusively to the tourist and pilgrim travel sub-industries, and as Youell notes, "countries which have a significantly higher proportion of incoming tourists ... will have a healthy surplus on ... [their] balance of payments." When examining other major components within the travel industry such as business or family-related trips, the flows are either two-dimensional or are too dispersed to have a significant impact on the destination's local economy [141].

Sounds pretty, well, *scientific* doesn't it? But what is it really saying? Um ... yeah. It's hard to figure out. Once you translate it into plain speech, though, it seems like mostly common sense:

> One scholar showed that international pilgrims, like tourists, bring money into a country and don't take it out, which improves a country's bottom line. Money from business travelers, by contrast, flows in but also flows back out. Family travel, more widely dispersed, rarely affects local economies [Youell 141].

The original version was full of fake science—the writer was essentially B.S.-ing the reader. If the reader—the professor, in this case—prefers the absence of B.S., the grade will probably be better.

A better term for this faux-scientific way of writing is the "Objective Style," because it fakes being scientific and objective.

I: Style and the Academy

What we call it doesn't really matter; it's how we use it that counts. And we use it far too readily. The Objective Style *sounds* scientific, so it must *be* scientific, the reasoning goes. In fact, it's no more scientific than the fortune-telling of Professor Marvel in *The Wizard of Oz*. Rather than simplifying things, it adds a lot of seemingly objective mumbo-jumbo that makes them hard to understand. But most students come to college thinking that's how they should write.

They're wrong.

The Bad Guys: Prepositional Phrases and "To Be"

So, what's wrong with the fake-scientific paragraph? Three things. First, the writer picked a boring quote from her source. (We'll talk about how to avoid that in Chapter 16.) Second, the paragraph is full of prepositional phrases, and consequently reads like a shopping list of ideas. Third, it relies too heavily on the most boring verb in the English language, the verb "to be."

Let's look at the second and third problems here.

Writing a good sentence takes skill, but writing a list is easy. When we write in the Objective Style, we tend to write in lists, gluing them together with prepositional phrases and the verb "to be." Let's look at that paragraph again, this time reformatted and highlighted to illustrate the problems. Do you see how it's a list?

This formation
   OF one-dimensional flows seems
   TO apply exclusively
   TO the tourist and pilgrim travel sub-industries, and
   AS Youell notes, "countries which have a significantly higher proportion
   OF incoming tourists ... will have a healthy surplus
   ON ... [their] balance of payments." When examining other major components
   WITHIN the travel industry such
   AS business or family-related trips, the flows
   ARE either two-dimensional or
   ARE too dispersed
   TO have a significant impact
   ON the destination's local economy (141).

The writer uses ten prepositions and two forms of "to be." Prepositional

2. Blinded by Science

phrases work well for showing relationships, but they're hardly action-packed. And "to be," the most common and boring verb in the language, describes the action of *being*. Nothing really happens: things exist, they relate to one another, and then the reader snoozes.

Now look at the revision, which has far fewer prepositional phrases, and many more active verbs (*showed, bring, take, improves, flows, affects*). Here, a scholar's research *shows* us something. It may not be best-seller material, but you can read it without snoring.

Of course, you can never get rid of all prepositions and uses of "to be." They're crucial parts of the language. But you can pay attention to how you're using them. When you see them clogging up your paragraphs, it's time to start revising.

No "B.S." About

Richard Lanham's Paramedic Method

The Objective Style deadens your writing and encourages B.S. Here's a variation on Richard Lanham's brilliant "Paramedic Method" of revision (you don't have to be a doctor to do it) that will help you get rid of it, and write tighter, livelier, and more honest sentences. Use this method after you've finished drafting a paragraph, or a paper. Once you've got material to work with, go back and apply it. Eventually this will become second nature.

1. **Circle or highlight all the prepositions**

```
A common pilgrimage for Buddhists
in Japan today is a pilgrimage
visiting the Eighty-Eight Temples.
These prominent temples are located
in Shikoku, Japan. There is a total
of about 150,000 people a year who
decide to go on this pilgrimage by
walking, biking, or mostly riding
in coaches (Koller 12). The route
total to visit the eighty-eight
temples is about 1,400 kilometers
and on foot takes between forty
days and two months to complete
(1).
```

Figure 2.1. Circle the Prepositions

I: Style and the Academy

2. **Box or highlight all forms of "to be"** (see Figure 2.2)

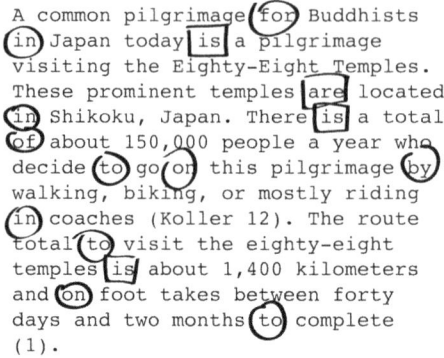

Figure 2.2. Box Forms of "To Be"

3. **Get rid of as many "be-verbs" and prepositions as possible.**
   Rewrite the paragraph; use simple, active verbs when possible, and complex verbs when unavoidable. Make things happen! Look for action in the sentence. Who's doing something? Whom (or what) are they doing it to? Try to rephrase your sentence so that subjects act, rather than just exist.
4. **Now, look at what you've cut out.**
   Have you lost any key ideas? Add them back in. Can you clarify by using transitions? Can you rephrase the main ideas in plainer language that shows what's important? You can't get rid of all the prepositional phrases, or make every verb an active verb, but you can cut a lot of flab from your prose.

Here's a revised version of the example in Figures. 2.1 and 2.2:

> About 150,000 Japanese Buddhist pilgrims visit the Eighty-Eight Temples each year, Koller writes (12). They walk, bike, or ride coaches along the 1,400-kilometer route. All told, the pilgrimage typically takes walkers between forty days and two months to complete [1].

One advantage of this technique is that it sometimes reveals that you haven't got enough to say. In the example above, a professor might ask, "So what? Why is that important?" We'll talk about the "so what?" question in Chapter 9.

3

Subject and Object

> *Most people are subjective toward themselves and objective toward all others, frightfully objective sometimes—but the task is precisely to be objective toward oneself and subjective toward all others.*—Søren Kirkegaard

Boring writing infects college essays because most of us know that academicians are supposed to be *objective* rather than *subjective*. But what do those words really mean?

To find out, let's start by considering some grammatical terms that help explain the Objective Style. This book isn't about grammar, but here grammar offers a good metaphor—a kind of model—that helps identify the problem.

In English grammar, a typical sentence starts with a *subject* and looks toward an *object*. The subject *acts*, the object *is acted upon*:

> I see her.
> We receive presents.

For example, in the sentence, "I see her," the person seeing—"I"—is the subject, and the thing seen—"her"—is the object.[1] In "We receive presents," the subject—we—actively receives something; the thing being given—presents—has nothing to say in the matter, and is the object.

An *objective* point of view typifies the scientific method: a doctor looks at a germ through a microscope and does things to it. He sees it not as a subject (a fellow organism with feelings and senses) but as an object—as a thing. And, when he reports on his study, he focuses on the object rather than his own feelings and responses. That's as it should be, and that's what good practical science should do. When you're reporting on experimental results and lab data, that's how you should write: no one typically asks for your opinion.

---

1. If *thing* seems too harsh a word, it's exactly what feminist writers complained about in the 1960s and 1970s when they argued that popular entertainment depicted women as "sex objects."

I: Style and the Academy

Conversely, a *subjective* point of view typifies good art: a painter looks at a landscape and interprets it. When he paints it, he's really painting how he sees it rather than exactly recording light bouncing off the object, as a camera would. When we see his painting, we see part of *him*—what he saw and what he thought. Doing so is only human. According to the famed religious thinker Martin Buber, we want our relationships with other people and the divine to be *subject-to-subject* (I/you), not *subject-to-object* (I/it); we are part of creation, participating in it, not separate from it and observing it from the outside.

Most topics for college writing move around, act, think, and do stuff, rather than sitting thing-like under a microscope. Professors ask students to write about ideas, books, facts, theories, stories, events, and opinions. They *want* subjective engagement, but they often receive papers written with fake objectivity, in the form of the Objective Style.

A student, unwittingly employing the Objective Style, wrote the following:

> In a modern world, where traveling is thought of as more of a leisure activity, taking a trip can still be an extremely profound experience.

Notice the "things" (objects) in the student's sentence:

- A modern world
- Traveling
- A leisure activity
- Taking a trip
- An extremely profound experience

All of these are nouns, verbals, gerunds, or noun phrases. Even actions become "things"—*traveling, taking a trip*. The sentence employs only one simple verb, a form of "to be." So, nothing really happens, either. Things exist, and that's about it.

A more subjective writer might revise it with the Paramedic Method (Chapter 2) and make the same point this way:

> These days, people may travel for pleasure, but they can still learn profound lessons along the way.

Here, notice how the "profound experience" springs from the subjects (people) who have it. The actions take the form of active verbs: *travel* and *learn*. The sentence says the same thing, but focuses on people doing things, not objects existing. What's more, it sounds as if a real person said it. It doesn't hide its subjectivity.

3. Subject and Object

So, what kinds of college papers can you write like that? Believe it or not, just about any assignment that asks for your interpretation or analysis.

Picture a spectrum (Figure 3.1)—of subjectivity and objectivity. Note that the most subjective item is *exploratory writing*. Writing like that means almost nothing to anyone other than the writer; it can be an important part of the writing process (Chapter 14), because it can help the writer think about what to say, but it's not really meant for anyone else to read. At the other end of the spectrum are *computer programs*, which are the most objective compositions you can write. If constructed correctly, they become self-sufficient things: they don't need you at all, they just do their jobs as little self-contained logical machines—in other words, *objects*. Creative writing registers as more subjective than *journalism, tables of numbers* as more objective than *description*. More important, notice that *academic argumentation* falls on the side of subjectivity, and *expository* (explanatory) *writing* falls near the middle of the spectrum. Most college writing dwells in that subjective neighborhood.

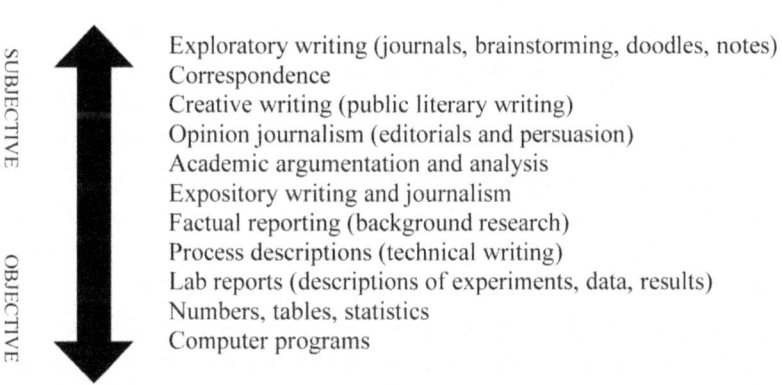

Figure 3.1. Spectrum of Objectivity and Subjectivity

Surprised? We're taught that college writing should be objective, but not that subjectivity plays such an important role. That's the "art" of applying the science. When we argue our main point in an objective research paper, for example, we're offering a reasoned and researched—but still subjective—conclusion.

I: Style and the Academy

Good writers know this, and they know that fake objectivity, like the Objective Style, isn't any better than honest subjectivity. In fact, because it's intended to create a false impression of objectivity, the Objective Style tells a kind of lie—it's actually less scientific. It's also harder to understand. So, the trick to good college writing is not to adopt the Objective Style, but to know when—and how—to look scientifically at data, and when to reason subjectively about it.

Let's not apologize for being subjective: computer programs may be objective, and see the whole world as ones and zeroes, but people aren't. We're not machines. Why pretend otherwise?

No "B.S." About

Subjectivity and Objectivity

It's possible for a paragraph to be both subjective and objective. Take a look at the following, from a dissertation about a poetry anthology:

> Davin's gossipy memo offers a good glimpse into the cautious mindset of an Oxford editor at mid-century: the opinions of persons in a position to attack or support the book are in the forefront of his thinking because they can dramatically affect its commercial and critical prospects. This is understandable because the anthology was part of the significant portion of Oxford's list each year that comprised trade (non-scholarly) publications meant to make money[10]—to subsidize, to some extent, the money-losing scholarly publications that advanced the Press's higher mission as part of the university and an expression of English literary culture.

The first part of the paragraph is quite subjective: the writer calls the memo "gossipy" (a subjective judgment), and describes what is in it. Then it explains the context argumentatively, contending that the anthology was intended by its publisher to make money—something that seems at first to be a subjective assertion. Ah, but then there's a footnote, which leads to the following explanation:

> [10] There was much precedent for this attitude. Oxford Vice-Chancellor Benjamin Jowett, who appointed members of the governing body, the Delegates of the Oxford University Press, instructed them in the 1860s that the Press had "adopted the maxim that to make money rather than to advance learning was the primary policy of the University Press" [Sutcliffe 59].

3. Subject and Object

The note thus provides objective evidence to support the seemingly subjective argument. It quotes from a history book and quotes the book's author explaining that the publishing house had a policy of trying to make money on their books.

The overall effect combines interesting subjective ideas with objective documentary proof. It is, at the same time, both objective and subjective. And, so, it's both interesting to read and convincingly researched.

4

Data

> *Life is made up of a series of judgments on insufficient data, and if we waited to run down all our doubts, it would flow past us.* —Judge Learned Hand

What could be more objective than data? It's the ultimate "object" in academic writing.[1]

Armed with statistics from empirical studies and surveys, many a Ph.D. on the tenure track has built a tidy career arguing about what the calculations show. That's because data fuels the modern academic machine—even things that might not, at first, fit your notions of what "data" means.

For example, consider Paul Blackburn's poem, "Good Morning Love":

> Rise at 7:15
> study the
> artifacts
>   (2 books
>   1 photo
>   1 gouache sketch
>   2 unclean socks
> perform the neces-
> sary ablutions
>   hands
>   face
>   feet
>   crotch)
> even answer the door with good grace, even
> if it's the light & gas man
> announcing himself as "EDISON!

---

1. Sticklers will insist that *data* is plural, as in the original Latin. In practice, many English dictionaries now sanction its use as a singular noun when it's used to refer to information in general. In scientific writing, however, it remains customary to distinguish between datum (a single data point) and data (multiple data points). Scientists often write about their results using the plural: "The data show…," "The data are…," and so forth.

4. Data

> Readjer meter mister?"
> For Christ sake yes
> read my meter
> Nothing can alter the euphoria
> The blister is still on one finger
>   There just are
> some mornings worth getting up
>   & making a cup
> of coffee that's all

Wait a minute, you say. That's poetry.

Indeed it is. It's also data.

Notice how Blackburn's poem offers *objective* details to consider—the time, the items in his home, the body parts, the meter-reader at the door, the meter-reader's words, and the blister. From this "data," these artifacts, we then try to deduce information about the *subjective* human being who's reporting them. What is he doing? Where? Why?

Perhaps he's waking up after entertaining someone in his room the night before, and sees items that remind him of it. Or perhaps he's waking up in a hung-over haze and seeing the world in a different light because he's in love. You could argue for either interpretation (or both of them!) as long as you have something to prove your argument.

Your proof? The data. Your data? The poem.

Most college writing works that way. It presents objective evidence, and then makes claims about what it means. There's no essential difference between how one academic writer argues about the implications of the numbers in a statistical calculation and how another argues about the meaning of the words of a poem.

In this guide, the broad term "data" encompasses many things; among them:

- **Texts**
  "The difference between the almost right word & the right word is really a large matter—it's the difference between the lightning bug and the lightning" (Mark Twain).
- **Numbers, Formulas, and Statistics**
  $ds2 = (-\alpha 2 + \beta i \beta i)\, dt2 + 2\beta i\, dxi\, dt + \gamma ij\, dxi\, dxj$
- **Facts**
  The Normandy invasion took place on June 6, 1944, a date now generally referred to as D-Day.

I: Style and the Academy

- **Ideas**

    Nietzsche characterized the individual's attempts to differentiate himself from the "tribe" as necessarily requiring struggle. "If you try it, you will be lonely often, and sometimes frightened," he wrote: fear and loneliness are the price of "owning yourself."

Each academic discipline approaches writing with slightly different expectations and conventions, but they all begin with holy regard for data. Economists argue about economic statistics and theories. Mathematicians tackle equations. Art historians study images and documents. Biologists compare DNA codes. Classicists translate old texts. Poets play with words.... It's all data.

Even personal essays rely on data. Events you've personally witnessed, facts you've authenticated, or interviews you've conducted—all data. If your testimony actually adds important factual information, you're as reliable a source for data as anyone else.

Wherever you get your data, though, once you've got it, you still have to do something with it.

No "B.S." About

Working with Data

1. **Be accurate.**

    Most good magazines and news shows employ "fact checkers" who make sure that their writers present facts that aren't mistaken (or fictional); in college writing, you're your own fact checker. If you're careless about facts, your instructor, who knows the subject better than you do, will probably sniff out sloppy scholarship or reasoning. When you include a quotation, make sure it's correct. When you copy figures into a table, make sure they add up. Don't rely on memory: go to the sources. If your notes confuse you, double-check them. Don't misquote or "misremember." Get it right!

2. **Give credit where it's due.**

    Imitation may be the sincerest form of flattery, and we all learn by imitating others, but academic writing depends on writers openly acknowledging their sources. Conventional formats such as MLA and

4. Data

APA styles require citations and footnotes so that other writers can build on your work, just as you build on the work of others. *Citations don't make you seem unoriginal*; they actually make your academic writing more authoritative. Failure to give due credit constitutes plagiarism, an offence that the academy punishes harshly. When you put another writer's ideas into your own words, say so. The scientific nature of academic writing—even student writing—depends on a "paper trail" that others can follow back to sources to test and challenge theories and conclusions.

3. **Don't expect data to speak for itself.**

   When you present data, use it. Don't expect it to do your work for you. If you present statistics, discuss what they show. If you quote somebody, say how the quotation proves your point. If you tell a story, make sure it functions to reveal meaning or frame a question. Don't simply string a bunch of paraphrases and quotations together, even if you properly acknowledge and document them. Put them into context, discuss their meaning, and explain why it's important to your argument.

   In other words, add some value!

4. **Make it flow naturally.**

   Learn how to integrate data into your writing so that it doesn't seem pasted in like scrapbook clippings. (This guide illustrates some specific ways of doing this in Chapter 13.) Remember to introduce your data, fit it to your own sentence's grammar, and then do something with the information. Think of yourself as the reader's tour-guide to the topic; don't hesitate to quote sources, or to paraphrase or summarize them, but always try to integrate them into the structure of your own writing so that they fit what you're saying.

5. **Distinguish between data and interpretations.**

   Don't make the mistake of taking the advice in (4.) about "natural flow" to the extreme of changing what the data means. Using data out of context or twisting its meaning to support your interpretation almost guarantees trouble—your professor will either assume that you're being sloppy and don't understand your sources, or that you're being tricky and trying to pull a fast one. Neither alternative is good for you. Treat data like holy writ: don't commit the heresy of distorting it to suit your purposes.

5

Specific Versus General

*It is impossible to say just what I mean.
But as if a magic lantern threw the nerves in
patterns on a screen…—T.S. Eliot*

If we had the sort of video projector that T.S. Eliot imagines—one that could, like an X-Ray gun, shine through us and project our thoughts for others to read—we'd still stand a good chance of being misunderstood. It's pretty mixed-up in our heads. Sorting it out takes work. Although we carry around a lot of information, we're still stuck with the writer's eternal question: where do I start?

Start with details. When you set out to write in college, your first challenge, before you worry about introductions, conclusions, and logical structures, is learning to get the details down.

The poet William Carlos Williams tried to explain the importance of details with his famous dictum, "No ideas but in things," meaning that a poet should avoid vague, general ideas and concentrate on those that reveal themselves through specific, concrete objects. But, since most of us aren't writing poetry, that still doesn't quite answer the question.

Here's another way to think about it: *Write in pictures.*

That sounds pretty smart, doesn't it? Unfortunately, since we have five senses, not just one, to cover additional possibilities, we'd need to add four more variations of the rule: *Write in textures. Write in sounds. Write in flavors. Write in smells.*

Now the rule doesn't sound quite as smart, does it? In fact, when you add all those other rules to it, it starts to sound sort of confusing.

What you're running up against here is a basic paradox that all college writers face—it's hard to be both clear and comprehensive.

Clear writing demands that your words be specific, definite, and concrete. "Be specific," your professors tell you. But when you use specific, definite, and concrete words, you're often not able to be as comprehensive as when you use abstract and general words.

5. Specific Versus General

Comprehensive writing demands that you generalize. But when you generalize too much, your writing gets so vague and dull that no one will read it—so it means nothing.

"No ideas but in things" is general enough to cover images, scents, sounds, textures, and flavors, as well as other obscure meanings, but it's confusing and requires some puzzling out and explaining. "Write in pictures," on the other hand, is vivid enough to get its meaning across very quickly and clearly, but it's so specific that it leaves out complexities, possibilities, and other important information. From it you might infer smell, touch, taste, and sound, but they're not spelled out.

Clearly we need to find a middle ground between the two.

To understand why this is, let's take a brief detour into semiotic theory, also called *semiotics*, or the theory of signs—an important academic discipline. According to one version of semiotic theory, a word is a *sign* that conveys information to us as part of a "semiotic triangle" (Figure 5.1) of *interpreter, sign vehicle, and referent*.

None of the three elements—the *interpreter* (you or your reader), the *sign vehicle* (the written or spoken language), or the *referent* (the thing referred to)—can do its job independently. For instance, texts in the still-undeciphered Indus Valley Language can't convey meaning since no interpreter can speak or read it

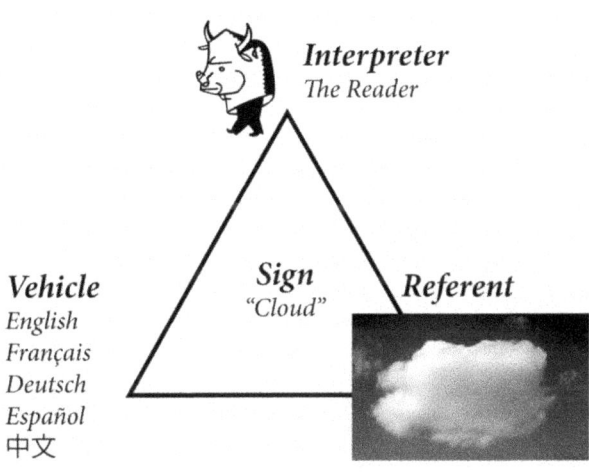

Figure 5.1. The Semiotic Triangle

anymore. When water droplets condense in the atmosphere, they have no inherent meaning—they just are, regardless of who sees it or what they're called. And a cow may see a cloud but not comprehend what it is, or know a language. Only when all three elements connect to each other does the sign "cloud" have any meaning.

So, what does this have to do with "specific versus general" and college

I: Style and the Academy

writing? Consider this. The construct represented by the semiotic triangle is one of the most amazing feats that our brains perform. No other creature on Earth uses signs the way we do. Even so, it takes those remarkable learning machines that we call "babies" several years to communicate intelligibly, and most of them don't grow up to fully master speaking and writing until they're in their twenties—or even later in the case of professional writers. Coding and decoding language is always hard work.

High-level abstractions make it even harder.

To understand the nature of abstraction, think of a toddler who comes in the front door crying inconsolably. You comfort him and ask him what's wrong. "I saw the cloud," he tells you. Okay, you say. So what's the problem?

You can see the problem in Figure 5.2.

Figure 5.2. "Cloud,"

There are many kinds of clouds, and the one our toddler has seen isn't the same as the harmless generic one you were thinking of, and that was illustrated in Figure 5.1. The toddler doesn't have the language to say what he saw—just the high-level abstractions that we learn in our early years (*cloud,*

5. Specific Versus General

doggie, pretty, and so on). But he knows what he felt when he saw it. By the time he's an adult, the word "cloud" will cover a whole class of meteorological phenomena—just one of the many thousands of abstractions an adult uses to tame the wildness of the world with language. To evoke in the adult emotions like those the toddler felt, a writer has to cut through years of experience abstracting and classifying things, forget the generic cloud of Figure 5.1 and, by vividly describing dark, billowing shapes, whirling winds, rumbles and cracks of thunder, and flashes of lightning, bring to the reader's mind the malevolent cloud of Figure 5.2.

So, on the one hand, we human beings are in the business of generalizing and abstracting things, as a way of managing the world. But, on the other hand, specific things get our attention, because the primitive animal who lurks around the base of our brains wants to know whether to fight, flee, eat, have sex, or sleep. It relies on our five senses for that information. When you want people to pay attention, you need to write in ways that appeal to those senses and instincts. To do that you must cut through the fog of abstraction.

Higher-level abstractions—words like "beauty" and "truth"—take in thousands of concepts and millions of specifics, but they're too general to tell us much. You've probably heard the instruction, "Show, don't tell." This is what it's about. A word like "beauty" tells us that something is beautiful, but a detailed description of a winter landscape shows us the particular kind of beauty in question. Subjective forms of writing, like poetry and creative prose, rely on such concrete sensory descriptions to transport us into the writer's world.

High school writing, on the other hand, mostly required you to *generalize*—to see the big picture, see how things connect, and learn to discuss abstract concepts. Generalizations were okay. College writing requires you to both understand the abstract concepts and investigate their specifics by applying them.

Most college writing exists somewhere between the two extremes. For instance, a scientist describing the weather phenomenon in Figure 5.2 might refer to *a Stage 2 cumulonimbus supercell, with prominent wall clouds and a mesocyclone producing a funnel cloud with tornadic rotation*. That's not exactly a poet's *deep rumbles of thunder and slashes of sun-bright lightning forking across a looming, plum-purple sky*, but it's specific and detailed. It manages to be specific and comprehensive at the same time. After all, your meteorology professor isn't looking for poetry that brings romantic tears to her eyes or makes her feel like a child caught in a storm. But she also wants to see detailed data, not high-level abstractions like *inclement weather*.

I: Style and the Academy

So that's the deal.

One word of caution, though.

As we've seen, the Objective Style (Chapter 3) tempts us to turn everything, including ideas, into things. You might think those things count as the "specifics" recommended here, but they don't. Remember: the Objective Style offers up fake science and fake specifics. The kinds of lifeless objects it produces aren't things that matter to most people—it would reduce the storm to *thunderstorm activity*, for example, which is vague and dull. That satisfies neither the scientist nor the poet. Don't give in to writing that way.

The best writers know whom they're writing for, and manage to be comprehensive while animating their writing with an active, living intelligence that takes those things and puts them into action. They use specifics that suggest or stand for much larger and more general meanings, and that back up their more general statements with examples that the reader can envision.

Fluent Minds, Fumbling Fingers

James Joyce famously wrote some of his novels using what scholars called the "stream of consciousness" technique. Joyce sought to simulate the way a mind thinks—through associations, images, smells, memories, puns, digressions, and stray thoughts. But decoding Joyce's "stream" into something meaningful requires hard work on the reader's part. Something that's supposedly flashed through someone's mind in an instant may take hours of study to figure out.

Joyce lived before cognitive psychologists knew much about how the brain functions. Now they tell us that even the fastest talkers or typists think a lot faster than they communicate. From birth, our brains use a kind of natural grammar that Harvard's Steven Pinker terms "mentalese." We're fluent in it. As we grow up, we learn to translate mentalese into English, and vice-versa. Even so, words remain a "foreign" language; a lot gets lost in translation.

To make up for this "bandwidth" problem, language uses shortcuts to keep up with our racing minds. Like Lord Bulwer-Lytton (Figure 5.3), author of a famously bad novel, we use abstractions to approximate our thoughts. A good abstraction can stand for hundreds, even thousands, of words and associations.

But abstractions are a mixed blessing. On one hand, we need them. How else could we talk about concepts like *truth* or *beauty*, or even *survival of*

5. Specific Versus General

the fittest, without using broad abstractions? We can't very well churn out the millions of things we know about those concepts each time we want to talk about them. We'd never get past the data.

On the other hand, abstractions tend to suck the life out of prose since they take the place of specifics that we can visualize and imagine. Instead of seeing Uncle Ed's *puffy red cheeks and purplish, pitted, drunkard's nose,* we're told he was *florid.* Instead of learning that one reporter made a *dumb factual error* in an article on gun control, we hear charges of *media bias.* Instead of *rain pooling in the corner of the window frame, wind howling, and dimly glimpsed branches rattling and scratching against the panes in the dark,* we get *a stormy night.*

Figure 5.3. Lord Bulwer-Lytton

The Trap of Abstraction

Abstractions are relative. For example, technical language can be quite specific, but it may use abstract words from Latin or specialized jargon that have little meaning to the general reader. By the same token, colloquial language can be extremely specific, but its terms are sometimes too imprecise or variable for technical purposes; so, for example, botanists prefer to refer to *Atirrinhum majus* rather than "snapdragon" when describing the flower.

Rather than thinking about specificity and abstraction as a purely good or bad issue, it helps to envision a circle (Figure 5.4), around which we can identify different kinds of abstractions and different levels of specificity.

Clearly, abstractions are necessary to writers, and we can't avoid them. But we can avoid falling into their trap.

I: Style and the Academy

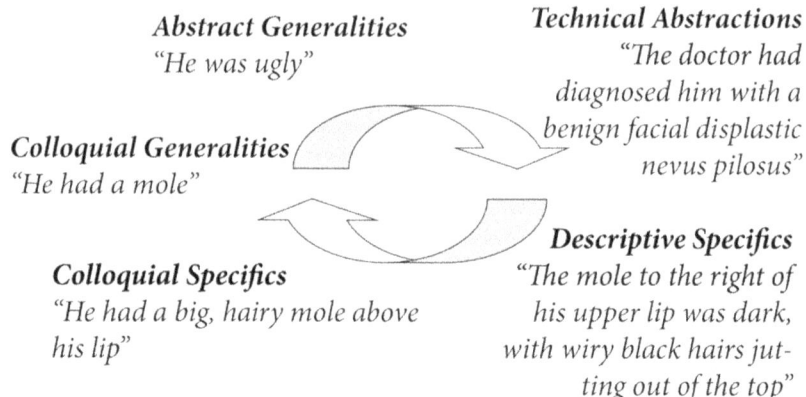

Figure 5.4. A Circle of Abstraction

When you write for others, you instinctively make your points tidy and presentable. That instinct can trap writers—unless you're careful, you'll end up generalizing and abstracting your points to death. Writing for yourself can help you avoid the trap. When you write for yourself, you have "permission" to be messy, untidy, and all over the map. And, when you're thinking on paper, that's just where you want to be. You'll find yourself generating specifics and details rather than generalities and abstractions. Then, when you shift gears and start writing for others, you'll have plenty of specifics to help keep you from falling into the trap of abstraction.

6

Active Voice, Active Mind

> *Alice was beginning to get very tired of sitting by her sister on the bank and of having nothing to do: once or twice she had peeped into the book her sister was reading, but it had no pictures or conversations in it, "and what is the use of a book," thought Alice, "without pictures or conversations?"*—Lewis Carroll

"Don't hide behind the passive voice," your professor scribbles on your paper. So, what does that mean?

First off, writing in the passive voice isn't wrong or ungrammatical: good writers use it all the time, and it is sometimes used in this book. Second, in college writing, you really can't avoid using it. So, if you find yourself writing in the passive voice from time to time, there's no need to hide your face in shame.

What is your professor complaining about, then?

Here's the thing: Unless you have a good reason to be passive—and there are many of them, some of which we'll examine below—the active voice usually makes college writing better. The dreaded Objective Style typically employs passive voice; techniques like the Paramedic Method (Chapter 2) are designed to get you out of the habit writing passively.

What, then, does your professor even mean by *passive voice*? Here's an example of a student's sentence that uses it:

> It is stated by the same Harvard Medical School article that "[m]ore than 50% of overweight young people have at least one additional risk factor for heart disease, such as high cholesterol or high blood pressure."

The phrase *it is stated by* makes this sentence passive. *States* is an active verb, but instead of being allowed to inject energy and action into the sentence, the writer has used *is*, a form of *to be*, as the verb. *States* no longer acts. It sits there passively and lets *to be* (the most boring and common verb in the language) do all the work. And what's happening? *A statement exists*—pretty

I: Style and the Academy

boring, no? To make the sentence active, the writer would need to revise it like this:

> The same Harvard Medical School article states that "[m]ore than 50% of overweight young people have at least one additional risk factor for heart disease, such as high cholesterol or high blood pressure."

It's still not a great sentence, but it's better because now that Harvard article does something—it *states*. In the original version, the action just existed passively. Nothing *did* anything.

Now, how could we make the sentence even more active and interesting? Let's look at it critically: *States* is a word that students love to use, but it's really just a more Objective-sounding version of *said*, which isn't very interesting either. But when you think of it, the article presents an interesting finding—that fat kids have health problems that put them at risk of developing heart disease. So how about a better verb, like *reveals*. Now something interesting starts to happen. The article reveals something.

We can even go a step further. The sentence quotes the article accurately, but the language of the article isn't particularly memorable. Suppose we paraphrased the quote, putting it into our own words, got rid of the dull statement of fact, and turned it into our own active paraphrase that showed what's important and interesting:

> The same Harvard Medical School article reveals that high cholesterol and high blood pressure affect more than half of overweight children, increasing their risk of heart disease.

That's a better sentence. Now let's figure out why.

As we've already noted, putting it into active voice makes things *happen*, and things that happen are generally more interesting to our brains than things that just exist. Second, in the revised sentence, the article *reveals* another action—that high cholesterol and high blood pressure are *affecting* something. That's two actions where none existed before, and action is usually interesting. Third, it does away with falsely Objective-sounding phrases like *risk factor*, *over 50%*, and *overweight young people* that just deaden things needlessly.

Okay, there's a bigger point to all of this.

Learning isn't passive, most of the time. At college, as you read your texts and write your papers, you're actively learning stuff. But you're not like a passive database, being filled up with facts to be drawn upon when you are called on to regurgitate them. You're given information to get you thinking and reasoning—making connections, developing theories, creating things, and arguing conclusions.

6. Active Voice, Active Mind

Most of the information that you learn in college is readily available out in the world. You could buy books to teach you what your professors teach, after all. It wouldn't be the same, though, as discussing the ideas in class with a professor and your fellow students. After all, a college degree represents something. It shows that you've made it through a process that forces you to think critically about what you learn. It also shows that you've been challenged by ideas, and have risen to meet that challenge. That, as much as anything specific that you've learned, makes employers want insist on hiring college graduates.

In other words, an important part of college is having an active mind and learning to think critically.

Writing well, without relying on crutches like the Objective Style and the passive voice, forces you to reexamine what you're saying. It essentially helps you practice being a better, clearer thinker.

Passive Situations

Not every sort of college writing calls for active voice, of course. The passive voice has its uses. Here are a few such cases:

- **To conceal agency.** Sometimes you want to conceal or deemphasize the agent of action, as in this sentence: *The administration is said to be considering salary cuts.* Who says so? Maybe you don't really want to say.
- **For rhythm and effect.** Sometimes the contrast between active and passive voice makes writing more dramatic, as is the case in the following sentence: *Name-calling rarely injures anyone, but bones are broken by sticks and stones.* Or a writer might show a character's snootiness by saying this: *He could not be bothered to be made aware of it.*
- **In scientific writing.** When you report on lab experiments and natural phenomena, you often focus on the effect rather than the cause, as in this sentence: *a solution of red potassium ferricyanide was crystallized.* (See Appendix 3)

If you're using passive constructions intentionally, and for effect, by all means keep doing so. Doubtless you have your reasons. In general, though, active constructions will make your ideas appear more thoughtful, lively, and clear to your readers.

In the epigraph to this chapter, from Lewis Carroll's *Alice in Wonderland*, a drowsy little girl gets bored looking at her sister's dull book, and falls asleep.

I: Style and the Academy

Academic writing rarely offers you the chance to include pictures and conversations, but by writing in the active voice, and making your prose come to life, you can keep your reader from snoozing off into Wonderland. Since your reader is probably your professor, that's a good goal to aim for.

No "B.S." About

Characters in College Writing

Most college writing should be in the active voice. Easy said, but you're probably asking, "How do I do it?"

Try thinking like a novelist. A novelist typically engages her readers by creating memorable characters whom we follow through the plot of a story. Since we're interested in those characters, we keep reading to find out what happens to them.

Believe it or not, you can do the same thing with academic writing. In fact, you're probably already doing it, but the "characters" are hidden by passive voice and the Objective Style. Here's an example from a student paper:

> Traditionally in Medieval pilgrimages preparation for the journey was to take care of very practical matters such as paying off debts, buying supplies for the journey or maybe even writing a will in case you don't return.

Okay, where are the characters in that? Can you see them? They're hidden. The sentence is about pilgrimages. So, who takes pilgrimages? *Pilgrims!* Now, let's rewrite the sentence so that it is about pilgrims:

> Traditionally, medieval pilgrims prepared for their journey by taking care of practical matters such as paying off debts, buying supplies, or maybe even writing a will in case they didn't return.

By putting a character in the sentence—someone *doing* something—suddenly everything becomes more active. Not only that, it also becomes more concise (31 words instead of 37).

So, make your sentences more active by telling a story:

- Turn your sources, ideas, and subjects into your "characters."
- Frame them as you would a story: *character > action > goal* (subject > verb > object).
- Omit as many prepositional phrases and uses of "to be" as possible (see Chapter 2).

7

Rhythm and Emphasis

> *Express co-ordinate ideas in similar form. This principle, that of parallel construction, requires that expressions of similar content and function should be outwardly similar. The likeness of form enables the reader to recognize more readily the likeness of content and function. Familiar instances from the Bible are the Ten Commandments, the Beatitudes, and the petitions of the Lord's Prayer.—William Strunk, Jr.*

This book's got rhythm, in case you hadn't noticed. it's got a beat, a groove, a bass kick all its own. That rhythm pulses through these words, chapter after chapter.

How can you tell? Just go back and look at the chapters before this one. Notice how each one starts with a chapter number, a title, and a thematic epigraph? They all start out the same way, but each says something different. That pattern forms a rhythm. By now you're used to it, and you know what to expect.

Now suppose, instead of breaking things up rhythmically into topics and chapters, your author had just written one long, gray column of prose with no dividers, no markers, no paragraph breaks, and no punctuation. Suppose instead of introducing each point with a contextual discussion, like this one, he'd just rolled from random observation to random observation, leaving it up to you to decide where "Subject and Object" left off and where "Data" began.

It would be slow slogging without rhythm, wouldn't it? But that's just one kind of rhythm.

Rhythm as a Guide

As readers, we depend on the conventional rhythms and patterns of written English to help us understand a writer's message. By making some things the same, we call attention to what's different. The structural rhythm

I: Style and the Academy

becomes a kind of guide for the reader, just as the beat of a song provides a structure on which the songwriter can hang lyrics, and the rectangle of a screen provides a frame within which the movie director can compose the way he shows us the world.

In writing, rhythm and structure show up not only in the large elements, like chapters, but within sentences and paragraphs as well. They serve the same function there—to help the reader. A good writer typically builds his sentences and paragraphs out of parallel elements, adding one to the next, showing how one idea connects with another, until the overall point becomes clear.

Rhythm Within a Composition

Let's examine a famous example of this: the "Gettysburg Address" by Abraham Lincoln. You already know how it begins:

> Four score and seven years ago our fathers brought forth, upon this continent, a **new nation, conceived** in Liberty, and **dedicated** to the proposition that all men are created equal.

Look how the introductory part of the first sentence points to two elements that parallel each other: (1) *Eighty-seven years ago, the founding fathers produced* (a) *a nation conceived in liberty,* and (b) *a nation dedicated to human equality.*

Now, in the second paragraph, look how Mr. Lincoln's sentences build upon those elements, parallel them, and introduce new parallels (the typography emphasizes some parallels, to help you see):

> Now *we are engaged* in a great civil war, testing whether **that nation**, or **any nation**, so **conceived**, and so **dedicated**, can long endure. *We are met* here on a great battlefield of that war. We have come **to dedicate** a portion of it as a final resting place for those who here GAVE THEIR LIVES that that nation MIGHT LIVE. It is altogether fitting and proper that *we should do this.*

The concluding paragraph takes those parallel elements, builds upon them, and leads the reader to an inevitable but wholly unexpected conclusion, introducing dramatic new elements in the same structural framework as Mr. Lincoln makes his point:

> But in a larger sense we **can not dedicate**—we **can not consecrate**—we **can not hallow** this ground. The brave men, LIVING and dead, who struggled, here, **have consecrated** it far above our poor power to add or detract. The world will little note, nor long remember, what *we say here*, but can never forget *what they*

7. Rhythm and Emphasis

did here. **It is** *for us*, THE LIVING, rather **to be dedicated here** to the unfinished work which they have, thus far, so nobly carried on. **It is rather** *for us* **to be here dedicated** to the great task remaining before us—that from THESE HONORED DEAD we take increased **devotion** to that cause for which they here gave the last full measure of **devotion**—*that we here* highly resolve that THESE DEAD shall not have DIED in vain; that **this nation** shall have a NEW BIRTH of freedom; and that **this government** *of the people, by the people, for the people*, shall not PERISH from the earth.

Your professors don't expect you to write like Abe Lincoln. (It would be nice, but they don't expect it.) Lincoln's technique has plenty to teach you, though. The rhythmic language that he used in the Gettysburg Address wasn't all that complicated, it was just particularly well done. Here's the good news: you can learn the technique too.

By now, you're probably wondering how to tell the difference between parallel structure—a good thing—and boring repetition—a bad thing. Try thinking of it as the difference between driving around in circles when you're lost, and driving around in circles when you're racing in the Daytona 500.[1] It's all a matter of emphasis—of going in circles on purpose, rather than by accident, and doing so in a controlled way.

Emphasis: First and Last Things

The point of the parallelism isn't to make everything sound the same, but to show off the differences between similar things. As the legendary writing teacher William Strunk, Jr. (of *Strunk & White* fame) noted in the passage at the beginning of this chapter, parallel structure serves to help the reader by calling attention to parallel ideas. The repetitions function like a kind of road map, so the reader knows where to expect the sentence or paragraph to lead.

Your obligation as a writer is to make sure that the parallels function consistently, and that you don't draw a map that leads the reader to expect a parallelism only to find that one never shows up. Of course, like any good writing technique, it's possible to overuse it, but if you're paying attention, that's not likely.

---

1. Look at the second sentence in the paragraph, for example. It introduces two parallel elements—driving while lost and racing in the Daytona 500. The second element, which is more interesting and exciting, gets all the emphasis, so it seems to turn the first element on its head. Lincoln does the same thing, only in a more sophisticated way, in the Gettysburg Address.

I: Style and the Academy

One rule to remember about lists and parallel structure is that when you use several parallel elements together, you should pay attention to two of the elements in particular:

- the first, *and*
- the last.

Think of Lincoln's short speech. Which are the phrases from it that you already knew before you read it? The first—"Four score and seven years ago"—and the last—"government of the people, by the people, and for the people." That's no accident.

The same principle holds true equally for essays and for lists (even humorous "Top Ten" lists, where the best jokes are usually at the beginning and end). When you emphasize the beginning and the end you help your reader bracket what you have to say, and make sense of it. He (or she) will naturally be paying more attention then anyway.

Since your introduction and your conclusion are naturally the most emphatic parts of your essays, you might as well put your best writing there. The same holds true for your paragraphs: they should begin and end emphatically. Even your sentences can benefit from the principle—begin forcefully, and make the last words pop.

That's the good news.

The bad news is that there's no simple formula that you can memorize to learn how to use rhythmic repetition and parallel structure. A writer only gets it from reading the work of other good writers, like Lincoln. Make a point of watching for it when you're reading, and you'll soon start to see it in good writing everywhere. Once you get a feel for the rhythm, you'll get the hang of using it yourself. And then you might start seeing checkmarks on your own essays, with odd professorial comments like, "Well put!"

No "B.S." About

Parallel Structure

Parallel structure, or parallelism, makes your writing more rhythmic, easier to understand, and more concise. When you're revising, look for ways to emphasize parallelisms. Here are some questions to ask yourself:

7. *Rhythm and Emphasis*

- Are "and" and "or" phrases expressed in parallel ways? If not, make them parallel:

    Tourists **spend money** and **demand services**.
    Not
    Tourists spend money and they also demand services.

- Are lists presented in parallel ways? Make sure they are. (Notice how each item in this list begins with a question.)
- Are you developing a series of parallel ideas? Make sure they're expressed in parallel form.
- Can you hear rhythm in your writing? Listen for similar sounds and tenses. If something breaks that rhythm, should it be expressed in a parallel way to enhance rhythm?
- Is your paper's structure parallel? A longer paper can be helped by being divided into parts, each of which begins in a parallel way. (See Chapter 21)

II: Argument and Persuasion

Or, Why Data Isn't Enough

8

A Jury of Your Peers

> JUROR 3: *Brother, I've seen all kinds of dishonesty in my day, but this little display takes the cake. Y'all come in here with your hearts bleedin' all over the floor about slum kids and injustice; you listen to some fairy tales; suddenly you start gettin' through to some of these old ladies ... well, you're not getting through to me, I've had enough! WHAT'S THE MATTER WITH YOU GUYS? You all know he's guilty. He's got to burn!*—Reginald Rose, 12 Angry Men

The classic Henry Fonda movie, *12 Angry Men*, invites us into the jury room of a murder trial. Over the course of an hour and a half, the passions, prejudices, convictions, and self-delusions of the twelve jurors spill out on the table for all to see as they argue about what's right, what the lawyers and witnesses said, and what to believe.[1]

Those twelve 1950s-era white guys sweating through their shirts might not seem much like you and your fellow college students, or the pointy-headed professor lecturing to your class about economic theory or mythology. Actually, though, they're a pretty good model for the way we look for truth at college. They enter the jury room, leaving behind the courtroom where a prosecutor has just argued for guilt, where a defense attorney has just argued for innocence, where witnesses have just provided facts (as they saw them), and where the judge has just explained points of law. Once sequestered, they must begin their own conversation about what they've just heard and seen, deliberate about what's right, and decide what to do.

When you enter college, you join a deliberative conversation too. It's one that's been going on since before Socrates drank poison rather than accept banishment from Athens, to show his students how serious he was about truth, 2,400 years ago. From questions of beauty, to the meaning and origins

---

1. Spoiler alert: In the end, of course, Fonda's tough, principled questions prompt the others to change their minds and find the defendant innocent. The facts just don't add up to murder. Even Juror 3, played by Lee J. Cobb, gets past his rage and ends up walking away from the courtroom feeling good about things. After all, justice has been done.

8. A Jury of Your Peers

of life, to the best way to fight wars or cure diseases, the academic deliberation seeks to decide which arguments make sense, which facts stand up to scrutiny, and which rules apply. You have to listen to the arguments and decide, then make your own arguments. Each "verdict" becomes part of the next "jury's" deliberations, and the conversation goes on across the years. Out of that conversation, we all come closer to the truth.

Learning the principles of college writing means learning to add your voice to that conversation in a way that will convince others to listen to you, and to your ideas.

Claims and Arguments

A court case begins with claims—assertions about the truth. Lawyers for the various sides stand up and tell a judge or jury what they intend to prove. Then they offer documents and the testimony of witnesses as evidence. Finally, they argue about how the evidence they've presented supports and proves their opening claims. All of these together make up an "argument." The jury's job is to deliberate on the arguments presented in court.

In college writing, the "jury" can be anything from fellow students, to your professor, or to the broad community of scholars who read published academic writing. Most of us think of college as a place where you go to learn facts. That's certainly part of a college education—many universities stress research and the process of discovering factual evidence. But college is also where you go to learn how to make sense of the facts, and how to make your own case for what they mean.

For the academic conversation to take place, contending ideas about the facts need advocates. That's where argument comes in.

So, what about that term, "argument"? When you think of an argument, you probably think of two drunks yelling at each other in a bar, or a married couple battling over who's to blame for not arranging for a babysitter. Okay, but if that's the case, why do we worry about it in college? The dictionary's definition offers some answers:

ARGUMENT [...]

1a. A discussion in which disagreement is expressed; a debate. b. A quarrel; a dispute.

2a. A course of reasoning aimed at demonstrating truth or falsehood. b. A fact or

II: Argument and Persuasion

statement put forth as proof or evidence; a reason. c. A set of statements in which one follows logically as a conclusion from the others.[2]

College writing is all about the second set of definitions—the intersection of reasoning and truth. And that's what our "jury" mostly does in college: argues about what's true and what's not.

Argument: A Three-Legged Stool

To understand argument, it might help to envision a three-legged stool, as in Figure 8.1. Like a stool, an argument rests on three legs. Take away any one of them, and it falls down. If all three are solid, it will support a lot of weight.

The three "legs" here are terms taken from classical Greek rhetoric: *logos, ethos,* and *pathos*. Good arguments have the support of all three elements, although certain legs sometimes bear more weight than others, depending on the circumstances. Let's look at each individually.

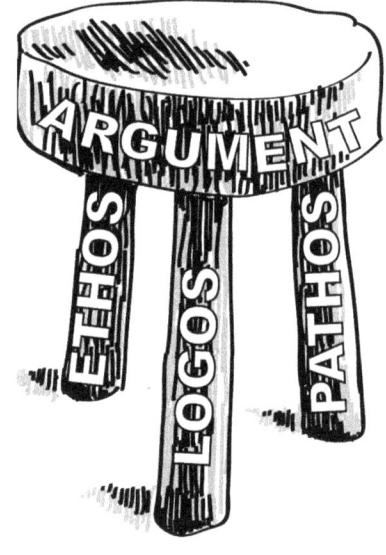

LOGOS—The Greek term for reason (literally, "the word"). It refers to the part of an argument that appeals to logic, evidence, and common sense to convince us. You solve mathematical problems using logos—it's all reasoning and deduction. Most of us don't base our lives on math, though, so pure logic isn't enough. Reasoning is the most crucial "leg" for college argument, but it can't stand alone.

ETHOS—The Greek term for morality (literally, "nature," or "character"). It refers to the part of an argument that depends on the character of the

Figure 8.1. A Three-Legged Stool

---

2. *The American Heritage Dictionary of the English Language,* 4th ed. Boston: Houghton Mifflin, 2000.

8. A Jury of Your Peers

arguer. For instance, if you think a writer is a liar, you're not likely to believe what she writes. But, if you're confident that she means well, you'll probably be open to her argument.

PATHOS—The Greek term for emotions (literally, "feeling" or "suffering"). It refers to the part of an argument that appeals to emotions. So, for instance, an argument can make us feel angry, or sad, or scared, even when it makes no logical sense, or when we don't much trust the arguer. Sometimes emotional arguments win us over despite our better judgment.

The art is in the mix, of course. Politicians, for example, tend to rely on pathos and ethos to persuade people—they make us feel angry, or proud, or amused, or fearful, rather than offering a dull lecture on the facts. But they use facts and logic too.

College arguments, being essentially scientific, tend to stress logos. But a college writer also has to convince a reader that he's done his research (thus demonstrating *ethos*), and has to write in ways that are interesting and emotionally compelling enough (thus employing *pathos*) to keep that reader from falling asleep.

Remember to envision the jury of your peers, deliberating over what you write. Like a courtroom, where law governs rules of evidence and argument, college subjects your essays to a high standard of logic and proof. But persuasion counts too: if your essays aren't persuasive, they don't get good grades.

And persuasion, it turns out, is a messy business.

Persuasion

Let's take a minute now to distinguish between argumentation and persuasion. They're connected, but they're not the same thing. It's impossible to argue without seeking to persuade. It is not, however, impossible to persuade without arguing—at least not in the sense of argument that we're concerned with in college writing, as the drawing of Odysseus in Figure 8.2 illustrates.

Persuasion isn't always noble and high-minded argument. In Odysseus's case, it takes the form of a quiver of arrows. In today's world it can include threats, lies, and flattery as well. At work, your boss may persuade you to follow his instructions with the threat of firing you. At school, your professor may persuade you to turn in your assignment with the threat of flunking you. At home, your boyfriend or girlfriend or spouse may persuade you with a raised eyebrow rather than a reasoned argument.

II: Argument and Persuasion

Figure 8.2. Persuasion. The Greek hero Odysseus persuades scheming suitors of his faithful wife that they are mistaken in supposing him lost at sea. Although Odysseus is a master rhetorician, here his means of persuasion isn't rational argument (illustration by Gustav Benjamin Schwab, 1882).

Hardly seems fair, does it? But who said life was fair?

Consider the following brief exchange from the 2000 presidential debates between Democrat Al Gore and Republican George W. Bush:

Gore: Almost half of all the tax cut benefits, as I said, under Governor Bush's plan, go to the wealthiest one percent. I think we have to make the right and responsible choices.

Bush: Man's practicing fuzzy math again.... After my plan is in place, the wealthiest Americans will pay a higher percentage of taxes than they do today.

Al Gore's facts were right,[3] and the reasoning of his argument was superior to George Bush's. From an academic point of view, he won the argument.

---

3. Media critics Kathleen Hall Jamieson and Brooks Jackson explain the technicalities:
> The problem is definition. Which taxes? Gore meant estate tax plus income tax. Bush meant only income tax. In other words, without saying so, Bush excluded a significant benefit the wealthy would receive as a result of his proposed repeal of the estate tax. What is the measure? Gore meant to say half of all the benefits of Bush's tax cut would

8. A Jury of Your Peers

Bush's response, though essentially accurate, told only part of the truth and didn't actually refute Gore. But, in the eyes of the press and the public watching the debates, Gore lost the exchange. How come?

Simply put, Bush's manner was more persuasive, and the presidential debates weren't being played by the rules of college argument. In the context of a televised debate, where nobody was going to sit down and weigh one set of facts against another, Bush used a rhetorical strategy designed to make Gore look silly, and few cared that his facts were weaker than Gore's.

Politics offers many such examples of how it's possible to persuade without the sort of proof that college requires. Voters usually decide based on their feelings, rather than rigorous logic. If Gore and Bush had been academicians writing papers for their peers, the story might have been different. Some might say that just proves that college argumentation isn't relevant to "real people": you've probably heard colleges called "ivory towers," cut off from reality, as if that were a problem. But the goal of college argument isn't just to win, it's to win and be right—to find the truth. Maybe it's idealistic to look at argument that way, but sometimes ideals are worth having, no matter how ivory-towerish they might seem.

If, by now, you're rolling your eyes, and wondering if there's any practical reason to learn argument according to the sort of Marquis of Queensbury rules that college teaches, think again. Higher learning has driven civilization forward for centuries, and it depends on the approach to truth that colleges teach. It's science, after all, and science has real-world value. Learning to prove your points on their merits, rather than through deception or intimidation, is itself a marketable skill in our world of ideas—it says something about you as a person that many potential employers value, and many professions reward.

The good guys don't always win, but that doesn't mean they're not the good guys.

Persuasion in Academic Writing

Don't take all this to mean that "persuasion" is a dirty word in college, or to suggest that if you have your facts right, you've done all you need to do.

cont. go to the wealthiest 1%. Bush did not dispute this claim directly but instead, categorized it as fuzzy math and shifted ground to claim that the wealthiest individuals—note that he did not say 1%—would pay a higher percentage of income taxes after his proposal was enacted than they did before ("Finding Fact in Political Debate," American Behavioral Scientist 48 [2004], 229).

II: Argument and Persuasion

Obviously, college writing depends on good "data," but for data to mean anything, someone has to read it. That's why good college writing requires not only a solid grasp of the facts, but a strong sense of style and presentation as well. Writing well only strengthens your argument.

Since before the days of Aristotle and Plato, philosophers have had to balance the ideal of seeking truth with the practical requirements of convincing people to listen to it. It's no different today. Academicians often fight heated battles in the pages of scholarly journals, competing to convince their colleagues that they're right and another writer is wrong. The academy sets rules that determine what's fair, but within the envelope of those rules, academicians play for keeps.

With that in mind, then, we will now turn to some ideas and techniques in the following chapters intended to help you put some arrows in your own quiver.

9

Who Says? And So What?

A lot of good arguments are spoiled by some fool who knows what he is talking about.—attributed to Miguel de Unamuno

You already know a lot of stuff. You'll learn a lot more by the time you finish college, but seventeen or eighteen years on this planet is a pretty long time. Along the way, you've picked up a thing or two. It's important knowledge, and you should be proud of it.

But… (You knew there was going to be a "but," didn't you?)

But no one cares now.

This is probably the hardest thing for new college writers to get used to when they start swimming in the big pond. All the things they've learned, all the blood, toil, tears, and sweat that they expended battling their way through high school and advanced placement courses will impress precisely nobody at college.

You see, everybody here—even your classmates—has done pretty much the same thing. And a lot of the people here, including all of your professors, have been through a lot more.

So, why should they pay any attention to what *you* have to say?

As a writer, your assignment, should you choose to accept it, is to make them care and make them pay attention.

Good writing can help you do that. But you need to learn some sneaky academic tricks first.

Who Says?

Until you become a recognized academic authority and world-renowned expert, your writing needs to come to terms with the question of how you

II: Argument and Persuasion

know what you know. This is an academic discipline known as *epistemology*, the study of the nature of knowledge. It's a branch of philosophy, but it informs a lot of college disciplines—particularly first-year writing—for the simple reason that learning to express yourself in college has a lot to do with learning to support what you know with data, good reasons, and logic.

A typical first-year essay begins like this:

> Throughout history, mankind has dreamed of flying.

This is an example of something that's probably true, and that you know is probably true. But how are you going to prove it? You see, in college you can't get away with making expansive assertions like that without someone challenging you by asking, "Who says?"

"Throughout history" not only shows that you haven't really done your research, it's a cliché. It's the kind of big, broad assertion that marks an essay as the work of a beginner. You can do a lot better.

As much as you know, you certainly do not know "all of history." If you did, you would probably be a historian somewhere, and not a first-year writing student. So, you have several ways you can respond appropriately to this challenge:

- **Study the subject**—You could read up on Greek, Roman, Chinese, and Renaissance works that discuss flight, and give some examples. It would be a lot of work for a freshman paper, though.
- **Quote someone who's studied the subject**—Perhaps you could find a history of flight, and quote that. If it's a reputable source, that would work.
- **Make a more limited and factual assertion**—You might draw on common knowledge, writing, *"The Wright Brothers realized the human dream of self-powered flight in 1903."*

    This still makes some general assertions, but also includes facts that a skeptical reader could easily look up, and comes across more believably.
- **Testify from verifiable experience**—You might begin your paper, *"I have always dreamed of flying."* Who could argue with that? You're the world's leading expert on you.

There are other approaches to answering the "who says?" question, but the main point is to avoid unsupported claims that call your expertise into question. Get specific. Write about what your research and personal experience have taught you.

9. Who Says? And So What?

Learning to solve the epistemological question is one of the basic tricks you need to master in college writing. Nothing marks a rookie paper more surely than empty claims that seek to make the writer appear wise and authoritative. Here's another example:

> Fad diets and detoxing programs can be detrimental to the user's health whether it's through abuse, improper use, or lack of sustenance.

Once again, who says? Why should your reader accept the word of a first-year college student that this is so? Here, though, the student has done her homework and is prepared to offer evidence to support the claim, so it's easy to fix:

> Recent news reports suggest that fad diets and detoxing programs can be detrimental to the user's health whether it's through abuse, improper use, or lack of sustenance.

By adding "recent news reports suggest" to the sentence, the student accomplishes several things. First of all, instead of the student being "on the hook" for the accuracy of the claim, the onus is now on the "news reports." If the reports are right, the student gets credit for citing a reliable source. If they're wrong, the student can defend herself by saying that she was just accurately reporting what was said. She can make it even more believable by citing a particular news source.

Second, "suggests" is one of those cautious attributive words that good academic writers love to use. Others, such as *claims, says, alleges, argues, holds, reports*, and so on, do much the same thing: they establish some distance between writer and source. This way, the writer isn't on the hook if the source's conclusions are wild, or improbable.

Here's a little secret about academic writers. They often make controversial and dramatic claims, but they hide behind a cautious, scholarly mask to do so. So, for instance, instead of saying, *the moon is made of green cheese* (which is just nuts), an academic might write, *a new theory proposes that the moon is actually made of green cheese*; the theory might be nuts, but the academic isn't.

What does this mean for you as a writer? It means that if you are careful to answer the "who says?" question, you can write about all sorts of wild and interesting things, and yet still retain the credibility of a cautious academic researcher.[1]

---

1. A word of caution: Ultimately, you're still responsible for assessing the credibility of studies and sources you cite. If you really write a paper claiming that the moon is made of green cheese, and turn it in to your astronomy professor, don't expect a good grade, no matter how artfully you attribute it to your sources. You have to find worthwhile sources.

II: Argument and Persuasion

Good academic writers learn to use a voice that is active, curious, skeptical, and cautious. Someone who writes like that has the freedom to tackle outrageous, radical, and cutting-edge material, and yet still seem a credible scholar. It's a good technique to master.

So What?

The other pesky question that academic writers have to answer is, "So What?" First-year writers often fall into the trap of writing a thesis sentence or a conclusion to their paper like the following:

> In this article Wallace included the reflections he had from the time spent on the cruise studying the individuals living the "pampered" lifestyle over the 7-day fantasy dream that everyone came to enjoy on the cruise.

This paper, which examines the writer David Foster Wallace's well-known essay about the travel experience aboard a modern luxury cruise ship, makes a thesis claim: *Wallace included reflections on the experience.* Okay, but so what? What did he think? What do you think? What are we readers supposed to take away from that observation?

In this case, the writer has taken the lesson about being cautious too much to heart. The thesis makes a claim, but the claim doesn't really tell us anything. Why is the fact that Wallace wrote about the cruise worth our attention? A better version might go like this:

> In this article Wallace reflected on his time spent studying the individuals living the "pampered" lifestyle on a 7-day fantasy dream of a luxury cruise, and found the experience such a dismaying indictment of modern life that he was ready to kill himself.

Here's the deal. College professors don't ask you to write papers because they feel like torturing you. They want to see you think, and to make connections to larger issues. In this case, the professor already knows that Wallace wrote about the experience of cruising. What he wants to know from you is something more: why it's important, and worth spending time thinking about. And, he wants to know what you make of it.

When you write your thesis sentence and your concluding paragraph on a paper, you should be sure to ask yourself the "so what?" question. If your thesis or conclusion doesn't answer that question, you've still got some work to do.

9. Who Says? And So What?

No "B.S." About

Common Knowledge

Sometimes the best answer to the "Who Says?" question is, "It's common knowledge." Academic writing puts a lot of emphasis on how you know what you know, and on properly documenting those things you've learned from your research. But what about the things that most educated people already know to be facts? You're not required to document those. Here are some questions to help you decide if something is common knowledge:

1. **Is it something that's so well known that no one is likely to argue about it?**

    Here are some examples of facts and data that can be considered common knowledge:

    - Dates of famous events, such as the destruction of the Twin Towers on September 11, 2001.
    - Famous quotations, such as Patrick Henry's "Give me liberty, or give me death."
    - Things that people commonly observe, such as the fact that the moon appears to be larger when it's near the horizon.
    - The names of well-known people, such as Charlie Chaplin, Stephen Colbert, Serena Williams, Martin Luther King, or Queen Elizabeth II.
    - Definitions of common words and derivations of common terms, such as the definition of "treason," or the fact that "verdict" comes from the Latin words for "speak truth."
    - Basic geography, such as the fact that California shares a border with Mexico.

2. **Is the "common knowledge" crucial to your argument?**

    The student example used earlier in the chapter, "Mankind has always dreamed of flying," might be common knowledge, but if it's important to your argument about the need for flying cars, you'll make a stronger case if you can cite a source, or attribute it to something such your own personal dream of flying.

3. **Have you used details that may not be common knowledge?**

    It may be common knowledge that the Japanese attack on Pearl Har-

II: Argument and Persuasion

bor took place on December 6, 1941, but it's probably not common knowledge that the commander of the Japanese carrier force was Admiral Chuichi Nagumo.

4. **Is it something you know, but that may not actually be common knowledge?**

   If you've studied a subject in high school, or another college class, it may seem to you like basic knowledge about that topic, but may in fact not be commonly known.

10

Claim, Warrant and Support

Spiritual life can certainly follow the pattern one sees in the fake martial arts, with most teachers making nebulous and magical claims that never get tested, while their students derange themselves with weird ideas, empty rituals, and other affectations.—Sam Harris

Claims

An academic paper is composed of a collection of smaller arguments, and each subsequent argument supports the others. If all the small, supporting arguments add up and make sense, the larger argument—or thesis—makes sense too.

Each of those smaller arguments makes what rhetoricians call a "claim." We've already looked at some claims, but now let's look a little closer.

In general, writers make four kinds of claims in an academic argument: claims of fact, claims of policy, claims of value, and claims of interpretation.

- **A claim of fact**—It argues about whether something is factual or not. For example, *If I drop a pencil it will fall.*
- **A claim of policy**—It argues that something should (or should not) be done. For example, *We should support and strengthen the Affordable Care Act.*
- **A claim of value**—It argues that something is of more, or less value than something else. For example, *The film* Citizen Kane *is better than* La-La Land.
- **A claim of interpretation**—It argues what something means. For example, *Donald Trump's election means people are tired of ordinary politicians.*

There are variations on these kinds of claims, of course, but most fall into one of the four categories. A typical paragraph may contain all four kinds

II: Argument and Persuasion

of claims: factual information that the writer claims is true, interpretation of what the facts mean, arguments about the importance or worth of the information, and suggestions about what to do with it.

Claims are a basic unit of argument, just as atoms are a basic unit of matter. Claims can be true or they can be false. Part of our job as readers (and as writers) is evaluating the truthfulness of claims. Those that are true, or at least defensible, make an argument effective. Those that are false make an argument B.S.

The logician and philosopher Stephen Toulmein developed a three-part structure by which we can identify and test the truth of argumentative claims. An argumentative *claim*, Toulmein said, is only as good as its support, namely its *warrant* and its *backing* or *supporting information*.

Warrants

We've discussed claims, which are fairly obvious. More confusing is Toulmein's notion of a *warrant*. A warrant is, more or less, a set of rules by which an argument plays. If the argument plays according to those rules, *supporting information* should prove it. Some warrants are quite complicated. Some are very simple. They are often unstated, and have to be deduced by the reader. Let's look at a simple one to demonstrate how a warrant works.

Take the simple claim of fact mentioned earlier, for example: *If I drop the pencil it will fall*. We all know this to be true, of course, and it hardly needs stating. The reason? Gravity. We all know that when you drop things, they're subject to gravity, and they fall.

But suppose we change the set of rules. Suppose, for the sake of argument, you are in a spaceship on the way to the moon. If you let go of your pencil there, it wouldn't fall at all—it would just hang suspended in space. There, the claim, *If I drop the pencil it will fall* is no longer true, because the warrant about gravity making things fall no longer holds sway when there's no gravity.

Here's a more complicated example. Suppose someone claims that *Abortion is murder*. This is what we call a claim of interpretation. The unstated warrant underlying the arguer's claim goes something like this: *the death of a living fetus in the abortion procedure is the deliberate taking of a life, and is thus a crime.* But that warrant is arguable. Someone who believes abortion is not murder might say that *murder is a legal term defined by law, and if the*

10. Claim, Warrant and Support

law says abortion is legal, then it can't be murder. Each side of the argument operates according to different warrants. Both can be defended. The argument remains unresolved.

Often when one arguer or writer attacks another's argument, that's what the attack focuses on—the warrant. If you can call the underlying assumption—the rules by which the argument plays—into question, then you've gone a long way toward winning the argument.

Supporting Information

The most extensive part of a college argument is typically its backing, or supporting, information. You'll spend most of your time and thought supporting your claims. With the example of the dropped pencil, no one usually asks for a warrant or supporting information. But, if they did, you could simply ask them to drop a pencil, which would demonstrate that the claim was true.

Most college arguments are more complex than that, and they draw on research, personal experience, and logic to provide supporting information. Let's look at another claim: *Tom Brady of the New England Patriots was the greatest pro football quarterback ever.*

To support this claim, the writer might gather statistical information about the number of times Brady's team won the Super Bowl, his pass completion percentage, his career passing yardage and winning percentage, and so forth. To back it up, she might bring in articles in which football experts discuss Brady's worth and compare him with other great quarterbacks. Finally, she might tell a story about going to a football game in New England and being overwhelmed by the love that Patriots fans had for him. All of these could be used to make supporting claims about Brady's technical proficiency, expert comparisons with other quarterbacks, and the extent to which he was loved and valued by his fans. Some of the supporting claims are factual, some are interpretative, and some are claims of value. All of them provide support for the main claim, about Brady's greatness. And, they might lead to a concluding claim of policy: *Brady should be elected to the Pro Football Hall of Fame.*

A college paper thus typically makes a thesis claim that is supported by claims about its warrant, and lots of claims about its backing information. Each claim-warrant-backing combination is subject to examination for its

II: Argument and Persuasion

logic and factual accuracy. As a writer, constructing arguments, you want to make sure each molecule of your argument holds together. As a critical thinker you can try taking apart the claims of others to see if they are as solidly constructed. That's called *analysis*.

No "B.S." About

Claim, Warrant and Support

As you're making and supporting claims in your arguments, here are some basic tips to keep in mind:

1. **Avoid big, grandiose claims that are hard to support.**
    Watch out for claims that will make your reader ask the "Who Says?" question. Instead of arguing, "Everybody wants a flying car," limit your claim to something you can defend, such as, "I want a flying car," or "As the many articles about flying cars featured in magazines like *Popular Mechanics* show, there's plenty of curiosity about the subject."
2. **Know your audience.**
    Remember that your fellow students will likely accept the claim "Students should be able to grade their professors" much more readily than a professor will. Consequently, you'll need to work a lot harder at arguing your warrants if you're trying to convince the dean to change school policy. Understanding the assumptions and attitudes of your audience is a key to good argument.
3. **Anticipate the "Who Says?" and "So What?" questions.**
    One mark of a convincing argument is that it anticipates naysayers— it refutes opposing points of view. This element of argumentation, known as a "refutation" (see Chapter 12), requires you to convince a skeptical audience that may be inclined to disagree with you. Your warrants and backing should bear that skepticism in mind.

11

Writing the Analytical Paragraph

When a truth is necessary, the reason for it can be found by analysis, that is, by resolving it into simpler ideas and truths until the primary ones are reached.—Gottfried Leibniz

Much college writing involves analysis of the ideas and writing of other people. While there's no single "approved" model for analysis in academic papers, it typically takes the form of analytical paragraphs—paragraphs that take apart and consider particular aspects of another writer's claims.

Whole books have been written about paragraph structure. Even so, you will probably find that a structure such as the "Basic Analytical Paragraph" of the following examples works well in the body of a paper when you're arguing from evidence. A typical paper might include many such paragraphs, linked by transitions and organized logically.

Both of the two model paragraphs that follow argue from data. In Paragraph 1, the technique is *analysis*—a taking apart of the data to examine how it functions. In Paragraph 2, the technique is *paraphrase*—interpretively restating what the data implies, and showing how it functions in a way that can be connected to the overall point of the essay.

The examples are helpful models, nothing more. You can adapt this basic paragraph for a variety of purposes for papers in the humanities and social sciences.

Basic Analytical Paragraph Models

Paragraph 1: Analysis

In Princeton moral philosophy professor Harry G. Frankfurt's popular 2005 essay, On Bullshit, he wryly observes that	• Introductory sentence that provides a context for the paragraph's discussion.

II: Argument and Persuasion

[o]ne of the most salient features of our culture is that there is so much bullshit. Everyone knows this. Each of us contributes his share. But we tend to take the situation for granted (1)."	• Quotation that serves as "data" for the analysis that follows.
Frankfurt goes on to suggest, like George Orwell, that "B.S." is a way of using language to manipulate rather than to communicate.	• Transition, the point ("topic") of the paragraph.
To emphasize this, the distinguished Ivy League professor employs language that conspicuously cuts through academic "bullshit" to make its point. His sentences are short, definite, and direct.	• Context for the analysis. Analytical discussion of "data."
When his vocabulary shows its erudition, as in his use of "salient," it's not mere decoration meant to impress, but because the word has a precise meaning he seeks to convey.	• Examination of a particular detail, and analysis of how it functions.

In Paragraph 1, notice how the writer "opens the door" to the subject of his paragraph with a topic sentence that leads smoothly into the data being discussed. It focuses on the data, rather than on the author's opinion and argument. The writer then presents the thing itself—the data to be analyzed—without further comment. It becomes a "fact" that anchors the paragraph in concrete reality rather than abstraction. Then the writer introduces his own argument: that the data proves a point. He concludes the paragraph by looking at specific aspects of the data (sentence length and word choice) that support his argument. The overall effect is of an honest and "scientific" consideration of the subject, even though the paragraph offers an opinionated argument.

PARAGRAPH 2: INTERPRETIVE PARAPHRASE

Wittgenstein once said that the following bit of verse by Longfellow could serve him as a motto:	• Introduces the subject of the paragraph, so the focus is clear.

In the elder days of art
    Builders wrought with greatest care
    Each minute and unseen part
    For the Gods are everywhere.
	• Data—a quotation from a poem.

The point of these lines is clear. In the old days,	• Transition. The point is not, in fact, "clear": it requires an argumentative interpretation, which Frankfurt will provide.
craftsmen did not cut corners. They worked carefully, and they took care with every aspect of their work. Every part of the product was considered, and each was designed and made to be exactly as it should be. These craftsmen did not relax their thoughtful self-discipline even with respect to	• Detailed paraphrase of the data, putting it into the writer's own words, and

11. Writing the Analytical Paragraph

features of their work that would ordinarily not be visible. Although no one would notice if those features were not quite right, the craftsmen would be bothered by their consciences. So nothing was swept under the rug. Or, one might perhaps also say, there was no bullshit.
—Harry G. Frankfurt

providing the writer's argumentative interpretation of what it means.

- Final point of the analysis, which connects it to the larger argument of the essay.

In Paragraph 2, taken from Frankfurt's published academic essay, the technique is less formal. The writer's intent is to restate things—to say them a new way that clarifies and interprets them. It too is analytical, because it too breaks the data apart. But its focus is on making ambiguous data clearer.

Paraphrase is a good critical thinking tool that many college researchers rely on when taking notes, because it forces them to internalize the ideas and make sense out of them, rather than merely reproducing them. Then the writer links his interpretive restatement to his larger argument. The overall effect is that of a teacher, making sense out of difficult data, and offering a "scientific" hypothesis about its meaning, even without point-by-point analysis.

Remember, when you write your own analytical paragraphs, that the point of including the data is that you're going to argue about it. It doesn't speak for itself. You have to tell your reader why it's important. To the extent that you can do this without seeming to lecture or argue, you convey an image of yourself as a reasonable, reliable "scientist" who is reaching conclusions after analyzing data, rather than as someone who offers loud opinions with no support.

That's why analytical paragraphs of this sort work well in college papers.

12

Classical Argumentation

Time spent arguing is, oddly enough, almost never wasted.—Christopher Hitchens

By now you're probably ready to start putting some of these tips and building blocks together. We'll talk about that in detail in Part IV, but since we've been discussing arguments, claims, and analysis, it's time to introduce the Classical Model for Argumentation.

For the last 2,000-odd years, most formal arguments have been built along the lines of a model proposed by the Roman politician and orator Cicero (106–43 BCE).

Obviously, in Cicero's day, there were no college papers, no printed books, no Internet, no letters to the editor, and no cable TV talk shows or talk radio. But there were debates and arguments aplenty, and many forums in which to match your arguments against those of others. Many of the techniques used by Cicero and his compatriots in ancient Rome are still used today.

Ciceronian argumentation was meant to be spoken aloud, by an orator, in front of an audience. As such it emphasizes certain things that aren't considered as important anymore when we write argumentative essays. So, we'll look at Cicero's model for argumentation, and then we'll look at a revised, modern model based on the same principles.

Before you start building your argument, though, remember the discussion of claims and support in Chapter 10. Remember that each of the elements of the classical argument is likely to be a claim or supporting data. As such, each part is a little argument in itself.

Ciceronian Model

- **The "Exordium" or Beginning.**
  The orator or writer begins by warming up to the audience, estab-

12. Classical Argumentation

lishing rapport, and announcing the general theme of the speech. This could be a joke, an opening anecdote, or a dramatic statement meant to grab the audience's attention. It often includes a thesis for the argument.

- **The "Narratio" or Narration.**
  Next the orator or writer presents specific circumstances or issues to be dealt with, a summary or relevant background material, and a discussion of what is at stake. This part of the argument essential tells a story relevant to the argument that puts the facts on the table. A modern writer might use it to introduce important data.
- **The "Partitio" or Division of the Argument.**
  The orator or writer breaks the argument down into the various claims and points to be proven.
- **The "Confirmatio" or Confirmation.**
  Here the orator gives the principal claims and support of the speech—the "good reasons" for accepting the thesis, or main claim.
- **The "Refutatio" or Refutation.**
  This is an extremely important part of the argument. It's where you consider your opponent's claim or claims, and disprove them. In a modern essay, it might be where you deal with skeptical readers who doubt your point, or with competing interpretations. It may also be something of a concession, where you admit that the opponent has some good points, but show how they can be refuted or dismissed without damage to the main claim of your argument.
- **The "Peroratio" or Conclusion.**
  Finally, the orator wraps up the various arguments into a summary statement, and amplifies the force of arguments already made. Writers today are usually taught to restate their thesis here. But see Chapter 22 for another approach that may work better.

As we've seen in Chapter 8 and Chapter 10, a college paper is a deliberative argument that makes claims, and although it's not meant to be read aloud or delivered to a crowd, the contemporary model for argumentation still follows the basic concepts of a classical argument: connect with the audience, lay out the basic facts, argue in favor of your interpretation, refute other interpretations, and conclude your argument.

II: Argument and Persuasion

Contemporary Model

- **Introduction**
A modern introductory section (it can be more than one paragraph, depending on the length of the argument) might start with a catchy opener, then tell the reader some of the background information, and close with a forceful statement of the main claim, or thesis.
- **Narration**
Like Cicero, writers use this part of the argument to tell stories and introduce facts that will be argued about in more detail later on. A writer provides background information, including personal stories and anecdotes that relate to the point. Unlike Cicero, this is where a modern argument might lay out its data and research.
- **Confirmation**
This combines Cicero's parts 3 and 4. It may outline the argument briefly, but it quickly begins setting out the specific claims and supporting them with good reasons, examples, statistics and testimony to prove the claims. This is where the writer makes his or her main points in favor of the thesis.
- **Refutation.**
The function of this remains mostly the same as Cicero's, and it's every bit as vital. Some writers, when they're arguing with another competing idea, may choose to make the Refutation Step 2 and the Confirmation Step 3. Either will do.
- **Conclusion**
The modern conclusion is essentially the same as Cicero's.

Don't make the mistake that a lot of college writers do and confuse this five-part argumentative structure with the five-paragraph essay you were taught to write in high school. They're not the same thing at all. A writer could stretch the five-part argumentative structure out over twenty pages, or a whole book, if necessary, with dozens or hundreds of paragraphs. Or, all five elements could be worked into a couple of brief, pithy paragraphs.

As you'll see in Part IV, there are many other ways to structure a college paper. But, if you're arguing in favor of an idea or attacking someone else's argument, the classical structure can still work well for you.

13

"B.S." and How to Detect It

If you can't blind them with brilliance, baffle them with B.S.
—*Anonymous*

Besides dull prose written in the "Objective Style," as described in Chapter 3, the biggest enemy of good college writing is what most of us would politely call "B.S." As Harry G. Frankfurt has argued, modern culture produces B.S. at an alarming rate, and most of us contribute to the problem—often without realizing it. Academic writers are particularly notorious for making B.S. seem like a respectable intellectual product.[1] It's as if every few minutes a shiny new idea shows up and dares college writers and critical thinkers to demonstrate why it doesn't pass the smell test.

Unfortunately, most B.S. sounds perfectly reasonable: it presents you with data, with claims about the data, with premises for considering the data, with detailed arguments about what the evidence shows, and with seemingly logical conclusions to be drawn from it. If you're not paying close attention, you're likely to simply accept it. But, when examined carefully, we find that B.S. typically depends on (1) bad data, (2) faulty logic, or (3) both.

Bad Data

Sometimes data is "bad" because it's just wrong—you add numbers

---

1. Not all academic writing is B.S., of course. Complicated ideas sometimes demand complicated arguments, an expert audience, and specialized terminology. Since a lot of modern scholarship, particularly in the humanities and social sciences, focuses on involved theoretical approaches to academic subjects, the terminology sometimes gets pretty opaque. The problem comes when scholars—and students—hide behind the jargon and seek to disguise their own subjective orientation by adopting the Objective Style, rather than risking criticism by writing clearly. If you've got nothing to say, clear writing tends to expose you.

II: Argument and Persuasion

incorrectly, gets your facts mixed up, quote old figures, or apply the wrong statistical formula. When that's the case, the bad data dooms any argument that depends on it; as soon as someone tests it, its credibility vanishes.

In college writing, this kind of bad data often shows up when you rely on memory for factual information rather than looking it up. For example, your essay's argument that the Mayflower Pilgrims became an important American symbol because they were the first American settlers won't impress anyone who's ever visited Jamestown, founded in 1607, thirteen years before the Pilgrims arrived at Plymouth Rock. Your data is simply wrong.

More often, though, data is neutral: it is what it is. It becomes "bad" when you use it to prove something it can't prove. Facts don't lie, but lies—or at least dishonest arguments—can use facts (and bad data) in an attempt to mislead or B.S. the reader.

Consider the following example, in which a 2007 poll by Fox News asked people the following question:

> Recently Democratic Leader of the Senate Harry Reid said that the war "is lost" in Iraq. Do you feel this was an acceptable thing or an unacceptable thing for Reid to say while U.S. troops are still in the field fighting?[2]

Fox reported that 65 percent of people surveyed felt Reid's comments were "unacceptable," while 29 percent found them "acceptable." What this meant, Fox's report implied, was that Senator Reid was badly out of step with American public opinion.[3] But was he? A skeptical blogger dug a little deeper into the poll and determined that the data didn't really support that conclusion:

> Of course, the phrasing is obviously about as subtle as a sledgehammer. Like all unreliable polls, the question is intended to produce a specific result (which [Fox commentators] can then use on the air). [But] just a few questions prior, poll respondents were asked how they'd describe conditions in Iraq right now. A combined 57% said we're either losing or have already lost.[4]

The facts here aren't "wrong": both poll numbers offer verifiable statistical facts—65 percent of people said they disapproved of the senator who claimed the U.S. was losing the Iraq war; yet at the same time, 57 percent of them said essentially the same thing themselves. But the 65 percent figure is "bad data" because it doesn't really support Fox's contention about the senator.

An honest argument from the poll's data might conclude that the public

---

2. http://www.foxnews.com/projects/pdf/051707_release_web.pdf
3. http://www.foxnews.com/story/0,2933,273673,00.html
4. http://www.talkingpointsmemo.com/archives/014219.php

13. "B.S.," and How to Detect It

had mixed feelings about the war: people felt uneasy about a prominent politician saying the war was lost, but simultaneously admitted he was probably right. Only someone intending to B.S. readers would "cherry-pick" the data to make the politician look bad. (It would have been equally misleading, for example, to trumpet the 57 percent figure as "proof" Americans wanted immediate withdrawal.)

So, can you trust statistics at all? Sure, you can, as long as you understand how they were arrived at. Inevitably, though, a lot of college arguments come down to arguments over how to interpret statistics.

Researchers depend on statistics to talk about large numbers. For instance, when analyzing a study of millions of data points, it's impractical to evaluate each point in relation to all of the others. So statisticians have developed many ways of analyzing numbers that, when applied correctly and consistently, produce reliable, testable results, and reveal important patterns and trends that might otherwise be hidden in the mass of data. At a certain level, only expert statisticians can truly evaluate the work of other expert statisticians, but most scientific researchers have to learn something about statistics as part of their training, if only so that they can keep each other honest.

The rest of us, though, aren't statisticians; we probably sympathize with Mark Twain, who wrote, "There are lies, damned lies, and statistics." We're stuck with using logic and common sense to test the conclusions. And that's okay.

Often, as in the case of the Fox poll, we don't need a degree in statistics to figure out that something smells funny; we just need a skeptical nose and a willingness to sniff out data that smells suspicious. Fortunately for us, where most college writing is concerned, logic and common sense turn out to be surprisingly powerful tools for detecting B.S.

Faulty Logic

Logic offers ways of testing the truth of statements. At its highest levels, logic looks more like the work of scientists testing mathematical formulas or computer programmers debugging code than of Ancient Greeks pontificating about the meaning of life. But just as we needn't become professional statisticians to read critically, neither must we become expert logicians.

Fortunately, logicians have already done a lot of our work for us. They've named and cataloged logical "red flags" that describe common errors. Rather than having to puzzle out the intricacies of formal logical proofs, most of us can get by with learning to recognize these red flags—known as *fallacies*—when they show up in our own writing, or someone else's.

There's a long list of fallacies, but in general they break down into three basic mistakes identified by Aristotle 2,300 years ago: fallacies of *Presumption*, fallacies of *Language*, and fallacies of *Inference*.

Fallacies of Presumption—This kind of fallacy presumes facts or connections, and takes them a step farther than logic can justify. For example, you know that racial tensions have historically complicated relationships between black and white Americans. But don't presume that racial tensions exist between two of your office co-workers, one of whom is black and the other white: They may be best friends or enthusiastic collaborators.

Fallacies of Language—This kind of fallacy uses terms incorrectly or ambiguously. For example, you might argue, "The children of a doctor get better health care than other children." A skeptic might say, "Not so. My next-door-neighbor is a doctor, and his kids are always sick." His neighbor, a professor of psychology, is a doctor, but not a medical doctor. By taking advantage of the ambiguous meaning of "doctor," but avoiding the merits of the argument, his claim doesn't pass the smell test.

Fallacies of Inference—This kind of fallacy makes a brilliant deduction or inference that isn't so brilliant. For example, you might safely argue that because Donald Trump was elected president, he must have been a charismatic politician. Charisma's a basic requirement to hold high office in our media-saturated culture. But it would be a mistake to infer that *any* charismatic politician will be elected president: many things other than charisma are required of a successful presidential candidate.

Fallacies as Persuasion

"Okay," you say. "That may be well and good, but in real life, people use fallacies all the time and no one calls them on it."

Quite correct. Fallacies can persuade very effectively, but remember that being persuasive isn't the same thing as being right.

All of those "attack ads" you see in political races are there for a simple reason: they work. They appeal to the gut, not the brain. If your objective isn't to discover the truth, but to make people do what you want, fallacies—

13. "B.S.," and How to Detect It

like lies—can work just fine ... at least until people catch on. But remember this: threatening people with a big stick can be very persuasive, too; it can influence people to do what you want. In the end, though, it won't convince them that you're right. College writing holds you to a higher standard.

After you leave college, deciding to persuade people fallaciously will be between you, your conscience, and your sense of how you want people to think of you. In college, though, the truth matters to your professors. It should matter to you, too.

No "B.S." About

Logical Fallacies

Whole books have been written on the subject of logical fallacies. This guide discusses fallacies in detail in Appendix 1, and gives some examples:

Fallacies Worthy of Skepticism

- *Ad Baculum*—Appealing to force
- *Ad Hominem*—Appealing to character
- *Ad Ignorantiam*—Appealing to ignorance
- *Ad Misericordiam*—Appealing to pity
- *Ad Populum*—Appealing to the crowd
- *Ad Vericundiam*—Appealing to authority
- Begging the Question
- Complex Question Fallacy
- Denying the Antecedent
- Denying the Consequent
- Distribution Fallacy
- Equivocation Fallacy
- Fallacy of Biased Statistics
- Fallacy of Insufficient Statistics
- False Analogy
- False Precedent Fallacy
- Guilt by Association
- Hasty Generalization
- Irrelevant Conclusion
- Narrow Sampling

II: Argument and Persuasion

- *Post Hoc* ("After, therefore because of") Fallacy
- Red Herring Fallacy
- Slippery Slope Fallacy
- Straw Man Fallacy
- The Gambler's Fallacy
- *Tu Quoque* ("You, too") Fallacy
- Two Wrongs Fallacy

Learn to recognize such "red flags" in your own arguments and those of others. If you see fallacies, it means the argument hasn't been fully thought through—or is deliberately misleading. By learning to identify B.S. in the form of fallacies, you can either make your own argument stronger, or pick someone else's apart.

NOTE: If you're interested in exploring fallacies further, pick up a good book about the principles of logic, or take a basic logic course. It will show you how to work through logical formulas in the way you would a math problem.

III: Research and Preparation

Or, Why the Librarian Is Your Friend

14

Writing for Yourself

Imagination is more important than knowledge. For while knowledge defines all we currently know and understand, imagination points to all we might yet discover and create.—Albert Einstein

The old saying warns you not to miss the forest for the trees. With writing, it's the other way around—you sometimes get so focused on the main point of your message, the forest, that you blind yourself to the specifics, the trees, that you need to convey it. As we learned in an earlier chapter, that's the danger of abstraction: you have a big idea (such as "truth") that tends to be abstract, and you must work at ways of making it more concrete and specific. A hallmark of good writing is that it makes its topic come alive with details, so that ideas reveal their complexities.

This chapter looks at some ways to get at the specifics. Some of them, such as taking notes and writing drafts, are things you may already think you're familiar with. Others, such as brainstorming or journal-keeping, may seem odd and impractical—until you learn to make them a regular part of your writing routine, and discover how much they can help you.

The most basic form of writing for yourself—and one you're probably already employing—is note-taking.

The Art of Taking Notes

Most students employ one of three basic methods of note-taking: the "Summary" style, the "Verbatim" style, or the "Map" style. Discover a style of note-taking that works for you, and stick to it. Good notes can produce great ideas.

- **Summary-Style Class Notes**—Rephrase and interpret what you hear, putting it into your own words as the lecture proceeds.

14. Writing for Yourself

This style requires detachment. You must both hear what the speaker says, and think lucidly enough to write a coherent summary while the speaker talks. Summarizing requires thought, and you risk losing details, but you often identify the big points more clearly and retain more of what you were taught. Here's an example from a religion class:

> Basic human needs: understanding, power, acceptance. Hebrews saw law as way to control world. Didn't always work. Concept of "theodicy" (divine good in evil world), illustrated in Job.

- **Verbatim-Style Class Notes**—If you're quick with a pen—or, better yet, a fast typist on a notebook computer—you may prefer this method, a favorite of journalists.

  Capture actual words that the speaker uses, as accurately as possible, in shorthand if necessary. Many who use this style soon find their fingers typing almost automatically, while their conscious mind listens to what's being said. If you use a laptop, you can paste parts of your notes into your papers, and rework them later—a time-saver. Here's an example from the same religion class:

  > Hum Need: To gain understg abt the world, gain power, be at home in this world. Destructive things happen, life is not just, innocents suffer. Personal tragedies, and they make no sense. To find ways to control evil. Hebrews, if they obeyed G's will, they wd be rewarded. What God told us to do. It didn't always work, the wicked did prosper, righteous punished. Theodicy. How to make sense of suf and evil in the world. Job. Why bad things happen to good people. Peop turn to faith to have the great questions answered.

- **Map-Style Notes**—If you're a visual thinker, you may prefer a note-taking style that's less "wordy" and more graphic. Some note-takers prefer to "map" a topic, creating a spiderweb-like chart of ideas and details. Figure 14.1 is a third example from the class.

- **Other Note-Taking Tips:**

  1. Be specific—Whatever method you use, get the details! If, for instance, your Art History professor lectures on *plein-air* (outdoors) painting, and spends fifteen minutes explaining why Claude Monet thought going outside to paint essential to creating an accurate "impression" of the moment, you won't be well served later on if your notes read,

  > Atmosphere important.

  But, if your notes say,

III: Research and Preparation

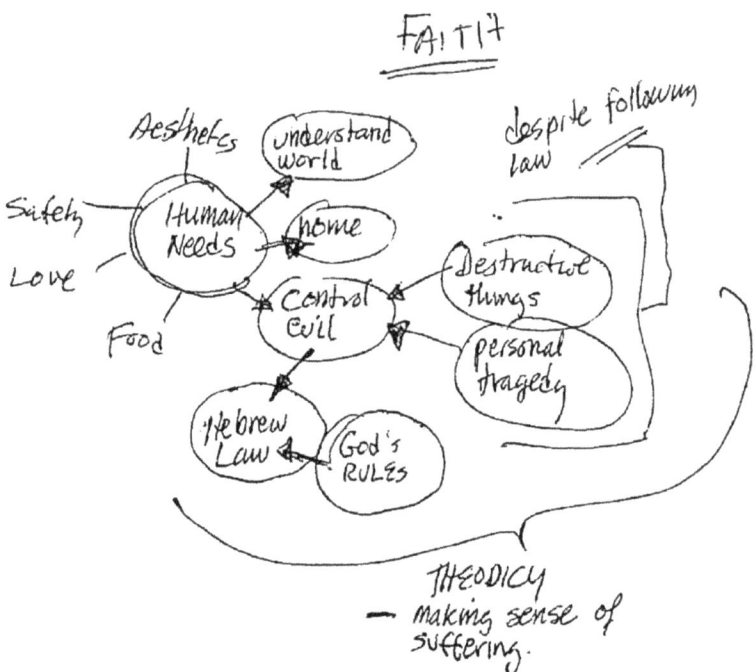

Figure 14.1. Map-Style Notes

> Monet: important to see subject as light changes during day—atmosphere gives subject its value,

you'll have a lot more to work with at the end of the semester, when you're studying for exams, or writing that Monet paper.

2. Write two-minute summaries—At the end of each class, leave yourself two minutes to summarize the day's lecture or discussion. Do this while it's still fresh in your mind.

3. Cut, paste, and scribble—When you read online sources, cut important notes and quotes, and save them on your own computer, or email them to yourself to work into your notes. With printed sources, forget re-selling that textbook! Mark it up as you go. Underline key terms. Circle important ideas. Jot down summaries in the margins.

4. Identify quotes—If you're jotting down notes from a library book, or someone else's book, be sure to use quotation marks when you copy down verbatim phrases from your sources! When you're writing a paper,

14. Writing for Yourself

you'll need to know which words were your own, and which came directly from your sources.

5. "Shuffle" notes—Index cards may seem old-fashioned, but they work. If you prefer taking class notes in a spiral notebook or on loose-leaf paper, that's fine, but make time afterwards to transcribe them onto index cards, each with its own subject heading. Then, when it's time to write a paper, you can literally shuffle the ideas like cards, and organize the various notes and quotes into the order you need to write your paper.

You can do the same thing on a computer file, using a word-processing program or a database program. Make each note self-contained, so you can "cut" notes from your document, "paste" them into a draft, and re-shuffle them like index cards.

6. *Prepare for inspiration* —You probably carry a cell phone in case a friend calls. Does your phone have a special ringtone for ideas, when they call?

Sometimes the best ideas arrive when you're not really thinking about your topic, as when you're chatting with someone over a meal. Make a point of carrying a handful of index cards, a pocket-size notebook, a voice recorder, or a portable text device. Equip your iPhone with an app to record audio notes, or a notepad for written notes. Get in the habit of using it. When inspiration strikes, be ready!

7. *Don't rely on recordings* —Some people tape lectures, which is easy with a smartphone. This is a terrible way to take notes. For one thing, it's inefficient (you essentially have to take the course twice). For another, it's passive: instead of taking the ideas from your professor and making them part of your own mental catalog of ideas by writing them down, you simply allow the machine to do the work. It's easy to forget the point of the lecture, and have the specifics drift away. You haven't done any work of your own to file the ideas away in your memory and imagination. The only way to get them back is to replay the tape.

And even then, you'll probably have to take notes.

Brainstorming

In business, successful creative teams often hold a "brainstorming session" where they bring people together and get them to start tossing out

III: Research and Preparation

ideas—good, bad, and crazy. One person's crazy idea sparks someone else's good one, and so forth. If done right, everyone leaves their skepticism at the door and no one worries about saying anything stupid; ten people come into a meeting with ten ideas apiece, but instead of 10 × 10=100 ideas, brainstorming multiplies the effect; it's more like 10 × 10 × 10=1000. Statistically speaking, you're more likely to find a really good idea from a pool of 1,000 than 100.

"Wait a minute!" you say. "There aren't nine other people in the room with me trying to find a good idea. I'm all by myself!"

Don't be so sure. You might like raunchy jokes, beautiful sunsets, bad puns, soap operas, chocolate, Mozart's concertos, Ultimate Frisbee, and hacking computers. You might like being sweet to children and being naughty when flirting during a date. But, when you sit down to write, typically you try to shut out all those other sides of your personality and just listen to the one that turns information into elegant sentences—the Editor, we'll call it.

Sadly, the Editor lacks imagination. It knows to leave the hyphen out of *anal retentive* and to add it to *anal-retentive proofreading*. But don't ask your inner Editor to dream up a good Halloween costume—or a good paper topic, for that matter.

When you're brainstorming, forget about that Editor! Write for yourself. Record as many specifics as possible. Don't worry about spelling or grammar. Explore as many avenues as your imagination opens up before you. Let all the different voices speak. Later, you can think about them more fully and turn them over to the Editor for cleanup.

In this context, brainstorming doesn't mean sitting in front of a computer screen, racking your brain for something to write about. It means writing for yourself, when there's no one else looking, as a way of generating ideas. Here are some techniques.

- **Freewriting**—Freewriting requires you to release the part of you that wants to control things, and just let the associations flow. If you're using a pencil, force yourself to keep the pencil tip moving, and resist the temptation to erase or scratch out. If you're using a keyboard, ignore the "delete" key. Don't worry about typos. If you can't think of what to say, say "I can't think of what to say." Keep the words flowing. By summoning up images, ideas, and specific details that flow into your mind, you'll generate ideas that lead to useful points when you sit down to write more finished prose. Here's an example of freewriting about the influence of the mystical discipline of *theosophy* on the artist Kandinsky:

14. Writing for Yourself

Since reading and thinking about Kandnsky and Theosph. Branched off in somany ways, I have learned and experience a lot as a result—but not wtoward my paper. & so…—I don't even want to think about K anymore becuase I don't know where to start … which makes it terribly difficultt o get a good paper together. Kandinsky's interest in spirituality largely defines his idea s of the role and fuctions of ar tand artest. His spiritual influences include Although primarily associate with the spiritual influence of Theosophy, K was never a member of the Theos. Soc. Nor did he claim to be a theosophist. Was probably more infl. by M. Blva, but his writings indicate other aspirations. Implicitly and explicitly.

- **Mapping**—Just as you might take visual notes in class (see "map-style notes" above), you can brainstorm visually. Jot down some key concepts, and then start drawing lines and branches to other ideas and details that come to mind. Again, try to be specific and concrete, with details rather than abstractions. Let the abstract ideas grow out of the specifics—don't try to go in the other direction
- **Word snapshots**—Imagine that you've got a camera, and you're going to take a photo of your subject. Try this even (or especially) if your topic is an abstract idea like "truth" (e.g., "truth in political campaigns"). What physical objects would the camera see (for example, political commercials, campaign posters, talking heads on cable shows, buttons, bumper stickers, and so forth)? What do those pictures lead you to think about?
- **Twenty questions**—Try a variation of the old game of "twenty questions" with your subject. The following technique, known as a *heuristic* (adapted from *Twenty Questions for the Writer*, by Jacqueline Berke), is a good way of learning something about your subject ; it can be applied to everything from a paragraph to the entire essay. Ask the questions, and jot down answers quickly. When you get through, you'll have a list of ideas and thoughts to work into your finished writing.

    1. What does it mean?
    2. What are its various features?
    3. What are its component parts?
    4. How is it made or done?
    5. How should it be made or done?
    6. What is its essential function?
    7. What are its causes?
    8. What are its consequences?
    9. What are the types of it?

III: Research and Preparation

10. How is it like or unlike something?
11. What is its present status?
12. What is its significance?
13. What are the facts about it?
14. How did it happen?
15. What kind of person or thing is he/she/it?
16. What is my personal response to it?
17. What is my memory of it?
18. What is its value?
19. What are its essential major points or features?
20. What case can be made for or against it?

Writing in Drafts

Experienced writers learn to develop their work by composing a series of drafts. Inexperienced writers tend to rely on their first drafts—maybe spell-checking a second draft, if they're especially ambitious. What do the veteran writers know that the rookies don't? They know that a first draft is usually not fit for public consumption

Except in an emergency, with a deadline breathing down the back of your neck, you should think of a first draft as a chance to shape your ideas and try out your words, but not as something you should turn in with a "finished" stamp on it. Again, the difference has to do with "writing for yourself" before you start writing for others. If your idea is to "perform"—to produce a finished work, right off the bat—your prose is more likely to be abstract and inexact. Or, worse, you'll never finish anything.

In *Bird by Bird*, her amusing and useful book of advice for aspiring writers, Anne Lamott argues for the importance of "shitty first drafts." Listen to the woman! When you're starting a composition, don't worry about what others will think about your writing. No one should ever see your first draft. It can be terrible, but it may give you ideas that you can develop. The trick is, once you've written it, put it down and come back to it later. Then, read it afresh—as if you've never seen it before. Does it still make sense? Try to see it with a fresh eye: what would another reader think? What ideas need developing? What parts do you like, that you can expand on?

Another benefit of writing in drafts is that you're more likely to allow the ideas to flow instead of self-censoring. Start out with a loose, informal, inexact draft, and build on it. Develop vague ideas with specifics. Flesh out sketchy arguments. Once you're ready, let others see your revised draft and offer suggestions. Gradually improve upon it—draft by draft—until it's something you can feel proud about.

Keeping a Journal

At first glance, the idea of keeping a journal for college writing might seem silly. "Today," you imagine yourself saying, "I began reading *Moby Dick* for the second time, and found it just as confusing as the first time." But a good journal is more than a superficial diary of events. It's a chance to turn what you think into prose. By reflecting on what you've read, and what you've done, you start internalizing what you've seen, read, heard, and thought. Writers traditionally have used journals as a place to try out ideas—the springboard to articles, books, essays, and poems. Why not use a journal for college writing too?

Try keeping notes on what you read, or trying out introductory paragraphs. Jot down quotations you might like to use sometime. Use some of the note-taking and brainstorming techniques discussed above to try out your ideas. A good journal is a safe place to experiment with any sort of writing.

Today, an updated version of the old-fashioned journal is a public "web-log," or "blog." Many writers use blogs like journals, as places in which to try out ideas and ramble on about subjects that interest them. Entries tend to be short, chatty, casual in tone, and unpolished. The main difference between a blog and a journal is that most blogs are published for all the world to see, although very few gain wide readership. But there's always the chance that you'll find readers out there who'll respond to what you post. Imagine that: an audience for your writing—what more could a writer ask for?

15

The eScholar and the Library

You could look it up.—Casey Stengel

If you're in college, you probably have an Internet-enabled computer in your backpack and a smartphone in your pocket. So who needs to go to the library when you've got Google?

You do. For now, the library's still a mandatory stop for college students, as you'll see shortly. But if you decide to go back to school ten years from now, it may be a different story.

Your author wrote this in 2017, in his office, on a laptop computer that connects to the Internet over a radio ("Wi-Fi") network. He could just as easily be working at a corner coffee shop or a bookstore. He has a smartphone in his pocket, which can also browse the Internet, and an iPad next to his bed at home. Who knows what will be available ten years from now? Maybe we'll all be able to surf the 'Net wearing high-tech sunglasses, like those in the *Mission Impossible* movies, and instead of typing we'll wiggle our fingers in the air in ways that haptic sensors on our iWatches can "read."

Today, the whole business of being a scholar is changing. Back when many of your professors went to school, everyone expected academicians to be walking encyclopedias, people so steeped in books and information that it was practically coming out of their ears. The professional qualifying exams required for advanced degrees typically tested how much one knew. But today, if someone asks you to identify an obscure line of poetry by a minor English writer from the eighteenth century, for example, you don't really need to carry the quotation around in your head anymore. You just need to know where to find it: click on Google on your phone, and the answer's right there.

The quantity of data out there already makes your head spin. No one can take it all in. In years to come there will be much more. Instead of simply memorizing facts and carrying them around in her head, the test of a scholar

15. The eScholar and the Library

may be her expert knowledge of the *context* of facts, plus knowledge of where to find them at a moment's notice.

So, what does this mean for you?

In some ways it raises everybody's expectations for your work. For example, say you're in a philosophy course, and your professor assigns a chapter on the twentieth-century philosopher Jacques Derrida, and the chapter happens to mention that his theories of language contrasted with those of contemporary "pragmatist" philosophers, but doesn't explain who they are or what *pragmatism* means in the context of philosophy. Back in the stone age, your professor might have cut you some slack if you didn't bother to trek to the library to learn about the pragmatists. Now, though, all it takes is a quick visit to Wikipedia[1] to understand the context.

You also need to know that different kinds of sources provide different kinds of information. For example, popular newspapers and magazines, like the *New York Times* and *Wired Magazine*, will give you articles meant for general readers without specialized knowledge in a subject. Government documents will provide official statistics and findings. And scholarly publications, like *Linguistics Journal*, offer expert peer-reviewed articles written by scholars for other scholars. All are available through your tablet and smartphone.

One thing's for certain. If someone asks you a question, answering "I don't know" is going to sound sillier and sillier as the century progresses. No matter where you are, you can always look it up.

Quality of Information

That doesn't make everything you can find on the Internet worth finding. One of your biggest challenges as an e-scholar these days is sorting out the good information from the bad.

Sadly, you can't rely on most of the information you find on the Internet. Google is a wonderful tool, and gets better each year, but it can't yet tell you whether a source is reputable or not. Let's look at an example.

Wikipedia is one of the Internet's most-used sources, and it's a fantastic resource much of the time—especially when you need quick background

---

1. That doesn't mean you should quote Wikipedia in your paper on the subject. As amazing a tool as Wikipedia is, it's still wrong a lot of the time. Use it to quickly learn the background of a subject; but if you need to cite any of the information in a paper, take the time to try looking it up in one of your library's more expert reference sources.

III: Research and Preparation

information. You just can't count on it. The people who write Wikipedia articles may be high-schoolers, they may be jokers, and they may have an agenda. But, interestingly, once they've gotten an article into Wikipedia, the article sometimes takes on a life of its own. There's a whole industry out there that makes its money by ripping off Wikipedia, and using the information on some other web site that sells advertisements or products. So, sometimes, when you find information on a commercial web site, it's really second- or third-hand *Wikipedia* information that may have been wrong in the first place.

Your challenge as a researcher is finding high-quality information, and not spending time looking through a pile of garbage websites slapped together to sell a few ads.

Fortunately, your college library spends tens of thousands, maybe even millions of dollars each year buying access to high quality information produced by scholars, experts, and reputable publications. Your tuition pays for it. That's where you should start looking.

Instead of high-schoolers and obsessed hobbyists, the online sources that your library offers to you are mostly written by recognized experts in their fields. Google offers you free information, and puts the burden on you to figure out whether it's bogus or not. Your library offers you information that is pre-screened by experts for its reliability and accuracy.

Who does the screening? Often it's done by librarians or experts in the field. Such information appears in what are called "peer-reviewed" journals. Unlike, for instance, newspapers and magazines, which are edited by journalists with good general knowledge but little expert training, peer-reviewed journals are edited for content by true experts in the field. The information in peer-reviewed journals is often much subtler and more specialized. It can be harder to use, as it's sometimes written in dense academic jargon, but it offers access to world-class thinking on the subjects you're writing about.

Alternatives to Google

Google often can't offer you certain sources because they're protected by copyright laws. Google's academic service, Google Scholar, will list expert articles for you, but unless you access Google Scholar through your library, you won't actually be able to read most of the articles. Instead, you'll be asked to pay for access. The good news is that your library probably already has

15. The eScholar and the Library

paid thousands of dollars for that access, and you can see the articles for free if you work through its systems.

Library resources aren't as easy to use as Google, of course, and you can't find things as quickly there. That's actually a good thing. Rather than give you garbage sources, the library systems make you try again. It usually means you have to think through your search more carefully. If nothing turns up, maybe you're not asking the right questions.

Increasingly, libraries are also offering services such as *Credo Reference* and the *Gale Virtual Reference Library* that are one-stop services meant to compete with Google for general information. The difference is that their sources are mostly copyright-protected articles that have been pre-vetted by scholars and librarians for quality.

Such systems and sources vary from library to library. That's where librarians come in handy. They're experts at finding information on their systems, and they'll teach you how to do it. Early in the term, if possible, stop by and get a librarian to show you how to search at your school. They can almost always find the time to help. And, once you've got the basics down, you're pretty much good to go.

How Librarians Can Help You

These days you can contact a librarian from your dorm room or anywhere you have access to the Internet. Most libraries have a "chat" program that lets you interact directly with librarians from the comfort of your home work area, and it's often available in the early morning and late evening. Librarians are also available by phone and, in some cases, by text message. Sure, it's faster to just Google something for yourself, but increasingly you can have the help of an expert with just a little more effort.

One of the hardest things about searching for information is knowing what to look for. That's one area that librarians can offer a lot of help with. A librarian can suggest *keywords* to put into your online searches—terms that are likely to turn up relevant information. And, they can help you figure out how to limit your searches, when a broad term such as "pilgrimage" turns up thousands of articles or books.

Finally, if you're working on an advanced project, librarians know how to get access to books and documents that aren't at your library or accessible online. Using a service known as Inter-Library Loan, you can get books and

III: Research and Preparation

documents sent to you from big research libraries all across the country, even if your own library is a small library at a community college. The only drawback to this process is that it takes time, so you need to give yourself an extra week or so in advance if you're going to use sources from other libraries.

Tip: Download PDFs When Possible

When you download articles and chapters from the library database, choose to download them in Adobe Portable Document Format (PDF) when possible. As we'll see in the next chapter, one of the key practices is learning to copy down the bibliographic information about the information you find. Downloading articles in PDF format will make it much easier for you later on when it's time to cite the articles in your paper. Many full-text articles are available in PDF format, and they mostly have the advantage of including the image of the page on which they originally appeared. So, when it's time to document where your quote comes from, you'll be able to identify the proper page or pages.

If the database you're using doesn't offer the PDF option, you can cite the paragraph number of the quote.

No "B.S." About

Searching Library Databases

In the examples below, suppose you're searching for sources having to do with the psychology of non-religious pilgrims on the famous "Way of St. James" to Santiago de Compostela, Spain.

1. Learn to use Boolean search terms, such as AND, OR, and NOT that allow you to combine keywords and names. Most databases offer an "Advanced Search" function that allows you to use Boolean operators. Use quotation marks for phrases: Pilgrimage AND "Santiago de Compostela" AND psychology.
2. Don't give up if you strike out at first. Instead, use broader search terms: Pilgrimage AND psychology
3. Don't use complete sentences, as you do on Google. Use keywords in

15. The eScholar and the Library

various combinations: *pilgrimage, travel, Camino, Santiago de Compostela, hiking, trails, backpackers, hostels, secular*. Remember that librarians can help you come up with the best keywords to use.
4. Use "truncation characters" like * or ? to capture variations in words. For instance, pilgrim* will search for *pilgrim, pilgrims,* and *pilgrimage*.
5. Start with general databases, such as *Academic Search Premier*, and the library catalog of books, then go to more specialized databases, like *PsycInfo*.
6. Learn to "browse" the online catalog. By using the Library of Congress Subject Headings, you can get a list of books in your library that are on or close to your topic:

> James, the Greater, Saint
> Pilgrims and pilgrimages—Spain.
> Santiago de Compostela (Spain)
> Spain—Description and travel.

7. Ask the librarian about how to find reference books. These are specialized encyclopedias and compilations on particular topics. Their articles may include bibliographies that will provide other sources. They're often in compilations such as the Gale Virtual Reference Library, but your library may also have actual printed volumes of encyclopedias to flip through.
8. Don't limit yourself to what you can find online. Libraries have huge collections of actual books that may be relevant to your topic. Not everything is available in a full-text database. Sometimes you have to go into the stacks and find a printed volume.
9. Think like a detective. The information is probably there. You just have to find it.
10. Don't hesitate to ask the librarians for help. It's their job!

16

Quotation and Documentation

He wrapped himself in quotations—as a beggar would enfold himself in the purple of Emperors.—Rudyard Kipling

On the one hand, your professor wants to hear from you, not from your sources. On the other hand, she wants you to back up your opinions with expert testimony and researched facts. But that raises a common student question: how much quotation is too much, or too little?

Think about it: why would you want to quote other writers in your paper? For several reasons:

1. Because they've said something interesting, in a really interesting way.
2. Because what they've said is data that you want to analyze as part of your argument.
3. Because they have information you need for your reader to understand your paper.
4. Because you want expert support for a point you're trying to make.
5. Because you want to show that you've done your research.

These are all reasons that students stuff their research papers and essays with quotations. Some of them are great reasons to use quotes. One of them, reason 5, is fairly lame. But they're all worth examining a little more closely.

- **Interesting, Brilliant Quotations**
  Sometimes, particularly when writing about literature, you quote someone because they say something brilliantly. This is a great reason to use a quotation, but you need to be picky about what you choose. Not everything is as brilliant as, for instance, poet Dylan Thomas's line, "Do not go gentle into that good night." Still, a well-known and distinctive

16. Quotation and Documentation

quote like that could add something to, for instance, an argument about the morality of assisted suicide or a personal reflection on growing old.

- **Data to Analyze**

    If you're going to analyze the way that Dylan Thomas writes, or discuss what he's saying in an obscure line, such as "Altarwise by owl-light in the half-way house/ The gentleman lay graveward with his furies," that's an excellent reason to use a quotation. Here, Thomas's words are strange, and don't speak clearly for themselves. You may need to help your reader understand your argument that the poet seems to be talking about a corpse lying in its coffin at a church at night.

- **Information You Need to Convey**

    Sometimes you need to give your reader background information. Suppose, for instance, you were writing about Thomas's essay, "A Child's Christmas in Wales," and you wanted to show that the author wrote it from the point of view of a child:

    > It was snowing. It was always snowing at Christmas. December, in my memory, is white as Lapland, although there were no reindeers. But there were cats. Patient, cold and callous, our hands wrapped in socks, we waited to snowball the cats.

    This is a lovely quotation, but unless you are talking about the language that he used, it's an example of something you would probably be better off paraphrasing: "Thomas recalled a snowy Christmas when he and a friend ambushed neighborhood cats with snowballs."

- **An Expert's Testimony**

    Sometimes, when you're making an argumentative point, you want an expert's opinion to back up your claims. So, in an essay claiming that Dylan Thomas could be considered a Christian poet, you might quote professor Bernard Kneiger's essay on the subject, which argues,

    > It is likewise obviously true that before an individual Thomas sonnet can be judged to be Christian or not, the "Altar-wise by owl-light" sequence must be understood as a whole.

    Note that Kneiger's sentence includes a lot of excess verbiage. The key point you want to convey is that he says the sonnet sequence should be "understood as a whole" before deciding about its Christianity. That's probably all you need to quote. Paraphrase the rest.

- **Showing Your Research**

    If you don't have anything to say yourself, filling your research paper

III: Research and Preparation

with quotations will not impress your professor, and it may do the opposite. *This is all quotations*, he'll say: *Where's the original thinking?* If you find that more than a third of your paper comes from quotations, it's an unmistakable sign that you need to do more paraphrasing and analyzing and less quoting. Paraphrasing will force you to put the ideas into your own words, which is actually a good thing. After all, your professor doesn't want to see a paper that's primarily cut-and-pasted together out of source quotations. He wants to see you thinking about what the sources say. You're writing the paper, not your sources. Show your research by doing something with it.

Stick to the Basics with Attributions

A mark of beginning writers is that they like to use the thesaurus to find alternative attributive verbs. So, in addition to the much-overused *states*, a rookie college writer will choose words like the following:

accepts	*charges*	*comments*	*exclaims*
believes	*declares*	*discusses*	*mentions*
expresses	*indicates*	*introduces*	*responds*
hypothesizes	*questions*	*remarks*	*assumes*
offers	*thinks*	*warns*	*considers*
acknowledges	*advises*	*answers*	*finds*
categorizes	*cites*	*compares*	*notes*
deals with	*defines*	*echoes*	*reveals*
illustrates	*insists*	*lists*	*assures*
points out	*realizes*	*replies*	*contends*
suggests	*uses*	*wonders*	*grants*
addresses	*allows*	*asks*	*observes*
challenges	*claims*	*concedes*	*shows*
decides	*describes*	*emphasizes*	*argues*
implies	*interprets*	*maintains*	*explains*
proposes	*reasons*	*reports*	*holds*
supposes	*utilizes*	*asserts*	*offers*
adds	*analyzes*	*concludes*	*speculates*

Usually this is a mistake. Stick to the seemingly boring verbs *said/says* and *wrote/writes*. If the writer is arguing, you might slip *argued/argues* in.

16. *Quotation and Documentation*

The others are mostly overkill, and you'll probably end up using them in ways that clash with their usual meanings. *Says* and *writes* become invisible: rather than being bored, your reader doesn't even notice them.

Also remember that you probably don't know what your source *feels* or *believes*. Those are interior, emotional things. You can't really know what your source *thinks*, but you can know what he *says*. What's useful to your reader is what the source *says*, or *writes*.

Incorporate Quotes Smoothly

One mark of an experienced academic writer is the way in which she smoothly incorporates what her sources say into the grammar of what she's saying. Consider the following, for example:

> Bernard Kneiger's essay argues that although parts of Thomas's poem are filled with Christian imagery, "the 'Altar-wise by owl-light' sequence must be understood as a whole" before being labeled as Christian poetry.

Notice how the writer works the quotation into the grammar of the sentence, so that if it weren't for the quotation marks, it would be hard to tell where the paraphrase left off and the quotation began.

You can also use [brackets] and the ... ellipsis mark to alter the quotation's grammar or shorten the material to fit your own sentence. For example,

> Thomas describes a place where "It [is] always snowing at Christmas. December ... is white as Lapland, although there [are] no reindeers."

Why Document?

As we learned in Chapter 2, academic writing is scientific. A basic rule of science is that experimental results should be reproducible. In other words, another scientist should be able to reconstruct your experiment and reproduce it. College papers work on the same principle: another scholar should be able to find your sources, read what you've quoted or paraphrased, and understand how you came to your conclusions.

For that to work, another scholar has to be able to find the same data you found. And that's why it's so important to document and attribute your sources carefully and accurately.

III: Research and Preparation

When it comes time to document your quotations and paraphrases with footnotes or parenthetical references, you need to be careful and fastidious. Your documentation should be clear enough that a reader who wants to hunt down the quote you used or the sentence you paraphrased can find precisely where to look from your citations. Remember that if your reader can't figure out where your material is coming from, you're doing it wrong.

NOTE: *Failing to document where you got your information from, either intentionally or by accident, is considered* plagiarism—*a serious academic offense. To plagiarize literally means "to kidnap," and academics regard it as the intellectual crime of stealing someone else's ideas. Punishments can range from grade reductions to academic suspensions or expulsions, depending on the school.*

There's no good reason—ever—to plagiarize. Being in college means you're in the business of borrowing the ideas of others and adding your own thoughts to them: be scrupulous about showing whose ideas you're borrowing, and whose facts you're using, and you can't go wrong.

What to Document

Appendix 2 of this book covers the basics of documentation styles, such as MLA, APA, Chicago, and CSE, and shows how they're different from one another. But here's a quick summary of what most of them require you to copy down when you're reading sources in the library or on your computer. Get this *for every source* that you use:

- The name of the author or authors, if available; if a source is a book compiled by an editor, get the name of the editor too.
- The title of any article (if it's in a periodical or reference source) you're citing.
- The title of the periodical, web site, or book that the material appears in.
- The date of its publication.
- The name of the publisher and the place of publication (if it's a book).
- The page or pages that the material comes from, if available; for sources with no page numbers, the paragraph number (or numbers) of the material you're using.
- The Uniform Resource Locator (URL) if the material is from an Internet source that has no other information about where it is published.

16. Quotation and Documentation

Most documentation styles ask you for two kinds of information: (1) An in-text citation or footnote/endnote that identifies the source and page number where the material is to be found; and (2) a full bibliographic entry, alphabetized at the end of the paper, that contains all of the information listed above. That way, a reader can quickly see where a quotation or paraphrase comes from, and then, by looking at the bibliography or list of works cited, find out exactly where to look in the library to find the original source.

Make a Documentation Sandwich

Students often agonize over how many footnotes and in-text citations to give when they're quoting or paraphrasing several pieces of information from the same source. Here's a tip that will help you keep from having to fill your notes up with the abbreviation "*Ibid.*" (meaning "in the same source") or your paragraph with multiple parenthetical references: Build a "documentation sandwich."

The recipe for the sandwich is simple. Like a slice of bread on top, your sandwich should begin with an in-text attribution that says whose writing the material comes from. Then, for the meat of the sandwich, you can include multiple quotations or paraphrases, as long as they're from the same source. Finally, like the slice of bread on the bottom, you end the sandwich with a parenthetical reference or footnote that shows where to find it.

Here's an example that includes material from several pages of a book on Dylan Thomas. Notice how it includes both quotations and paraphrases:

> William York Tyndall's *A Reader's Guide to Dylan Thomas* identifies sixteen of the Welshman's lyrics as "great poems" that belong with the best poems ever written. Critics have found them to be "things from the madhouse or the analyst's couch ... [that were] dense to the point of clotting, ... rich and strange." Some loved his work, and some hated it. Much of the resentment of it, Tyndall says, sprang from Thomas's roots in the lower middle class (3–5).

Even though the passage includes material from several pages, it only includes the attribution at the beginning and the parenthetical reference at the end. Everything sandwiched in between, the reader can assume, comes from those pages.

III: Research and Preparation

No "B.S." About

Avoiding Plagiarism

Plagiarism usually happens because of three reasons: (1) you're in a hurry; (2) you don't know the rules about quoting and paraphrasing; or (3), both. Whichever it is, there's never a good reason to plagiarize, and the academy treats it as a serious violation of academic integrity. Just don't do it: it hurts you, it hurts your fellow students, and it hurts the very essence of what a college or university does.

As you probably know, plagiarism means *using someone else's ideas or language without giving them credit for it.* It's as simple as that.

You may do it by accident, you may do because you don't really care about fussy rules, or you may do it on purpose to get a better grade. One way or another, if you do it, it's bad news. Not only do most colleges run plagiarism-detection software on papers these days, but your professors, who read lots of student papers, usually can tell when the basic character of a student's writing changes—a sure sign of plagiarism.

Why risk it? Respect yourself. Respect the system. Don't plagiarize.

Here are some tips on ways to avoid falling into the plagiarism trap:

1. **Take great notes**

    When you read a source, be scrupulous about distinguishing between your own summaries or paraphrases and direct quotations from your sources. (See Chapter 14.) If you are paraphrasing—putting your source's ideas into your own language—be careful not to accidently include direct quotations, unless they're clearly marked with quotation marks.

    If you're careful about quotes when you're taking notes, later, when you return to your notes to write your paper, you can simply copy your quotes or paraphrases into your paper without worrying about checking them against the original.

2. **Sound like yourself in paraphrases**

    Students get into trouble when they're trying to paraphrase sources because they stick too closely to their source's language. Remember that when you're paraphrasing, you're putting your source's ideas into your *own* language. It should sound like you, not the source. If it sounds like you, there's little chance that you've accidentally borrowed your source's language.

16. Quotation and Documentation

If your source uses specific terms that you can't paraphrase, be sure to put those terms in "quotes"—it's fine to mix quotation and paraphrase as long as you clearly indicate which is which.

3. **Remember to footnote or cite what you paraphrase**

Just because you've paraphrased your source's ideas, and put them into your own language, you're not free to omit the parenthetical references or footnotes that identify where you got the information. All information that you get from your research needs to be clearly identified.

4. **Use a plagiarism checker, if it's available.**

Some schools make plagiarism detection software available to students, as well as to faculty. If your school does this, use it! The software will find places where your paraphrases and summaries are too close to the original language of your sources, or where a high percentage of the text resembles another source. If the software flags a possible plagiarism violation, rewrite it so that it's clearly in your own language, or clearly a quotation.

5. **Steer clear of "paper mills."**

There's a dirty little B.S. business out there on the Internet that caters to lazy and dishonest students, and that will sell you papers on topics close to your own. This is the worst kind of plagiarism, and can get you kicked out of school if you're caught. Although these sites claim to be legitimate "research aids," no legitimate researcher consults them. Even if you properly cite and quote material from such papers, your professors will penalize you for using them. And, if you use material from such papers in your own, and try to pass it off as your own original work, chances are good that anti-plagiarism software or a suspicious professor will smell a rat. Don't risk it! Even the "A-papers" you can buy aren't usually very good, anyway, and you learn nothing from using them. You're only fooling yourself.

17

The Critical Lens

We see the world through the lens of all our experiences; that is a fundamental part of the human condition.—Madeleine M. Kunin

Even with great research and proper documentation, professors find many student papers boring. The reason? They've got good information but they're not saying anything interesting about it. They read like long lists.

Lists are boring. As we learned in Chapter Two, the Objective Style encourages students to write in lists, which is dull, dull, dull. But paper assignments sometimes encourage it. Go to the library and research your topic, your professor says. So you turn in a paper that is essentially a thesis followed by a list of supporting information that your research turned up. *Bo*-ring.

Here's the organization of the typical college argumentative paper:

An introduction and thesis
Some examples and arguments
- Item A from Source 1
- Item B from Source 2
- Item C from Source 3

A refutation
A conclusion

It's essentially a list. One way to avoid this trap is by adding a "critical lens." This means looking at your topic from a critical perspective or particular point of view. It can add a lot of interest to the paper.

When you employ a critical lens, you end up writing about two things: (1) The object you're examining, and (2) the critical lens you're looking at it through. And, from your professor's point of view, two things are more interesting than one.

Adding a critical lens to your paper makes it more complicated, more meaningful, and more interesting.

17. The Critical Lens

What Is a Critical Lens?

Adding a critical lens means adding a second subject to your paper. You are writing about the main topic you're researching, and you're also writing about the way that topic looks when viewed through the lens of another topic:

- **Through a disciplinary lens**—Economics, philosophy, mathematics, history, psychology, etc.
- **Through a theoretical lens**—Marxist theory, feminist theory, semiotic theory, cognitive theory, etc.
- **Through a reader-response lens**—How a particular group of readers, or a particular audience, responds. For example, a culture ("Arabic culture"), a demographic ("Millennials"), an attitude ("slackers"), etc.

Let's look at an example of how using a critical lens can change your paper and make it more complex and interesting.

Suppose, for example, you have researched the conservative lobbying and political action group Focus on the Family (FoF), founded by the preacher James Dobson. Your topic is political "spin"—how the group's message gets sold to American voters. An ordinary research paper would find information about the group (its history; its conservative politics; its use of TV, radio, and other media; how it is funded; what issues it advocates, etc.) You'd then talk about how it spins those messages when addressing voters. That would be a perfectly okay research paper, but it would be, in effect, a list of how Focus on the Family spins voters. Pretty boring.

But suppose you added a critical lens—a way of looking at the topic. Let's say you decided to study the organization through the lens of "marketing." Here's what an outline of your paper might look like:

Introduction and thesis about how FoF markets itself
Background on Focus on the Family
- Organizational history
- Political influence
- Controversies

Overview of Marketing theory
- The Four P's (product, pricing promotion, and placement)
- Macro and micro marketing
- Marketing segmentation

III: Research and Preparation

Application of marketing theory to FoF
- How it employs the Four P's
- How it markets to individuals and groups
- How it appeals to different segments of the market

Refutation and controversies
Conclusion

This would be a much more interesting paper for your professor. It would show you doing research on your topic, and also applying other research to increase the reader's understanding of how the organization functions. You would, in effect, be writing two different papers and integrating them. It would show more thought and expertise than a simple "list" paper.

The Big Picture

In a sense, this is what college is all about. You're not just being fed information, you're learning about different ways to interpret that information. When you take courses in history, or political science, or biology, for example, you learn to see the world through the lens of those disciplines. You start to see things like a historian, or a biologist, or a philosopher.

Even when we try to see through critical lenses, our understanding is filtered through our own "perspectives" or "lenses" too. No intellectual theory has ever truly led scholars to understand the world. We can each use our individual understandings or critical lenses to add more variety to our thoughts about the world, but these learned perspectives are relative, not absolute.

The various courses you take at college are aimed at giving you new lenses to see through. Applying these lenses in your papers means that instead of studying a subject in isolation, as a mere collection of facts and information, you're looking at it through a theory or a discipline, or from the point of view of particular readers.

That's what real research is all about. And it's what makes a college research paper more than just an exercise if finding and regurgitating facts. It becomes an intellectual activity, a way of bringing together varied subjects that inform each other, and seeing the world differently.

Now, wouldn't you prefer to read a paper like that? Your professor certainly would.

IV: Writing the College Essay

Or, Finding a Home for Your Ideas

18

The Open House

You can't invent a design. You recognize it, in the fourth dimension. That is, with your blood and your bones, as well as with your eyes.
—D.H. Lawrence

Mrs. Smith probably taught you to write essays in high school English so you could take the SAT and ACT tests and get into college. You got in, so, logically, you should be ready for college writing. Right?

If only it were so simple.

No offense to Mrs. Smith, but most of what she said about writing a college essay was … well … half right.

Four Ironclad Rules Mrs. Smith Told You About Essays:

1. Always use a five-paragraph structure.
2. Always begin or end your first paragraph with your thesis.
3. The last paragraph, your conclusion, should always restate your thesis.
4. The three body paragraphs should always be examples that support your thesis.

Sure. Sort of. If you obediently follow those rules, your college essays will sound like … good high school essays.

In high school, the challenge was simply getting you to write something—anything—coherent enough to show colleges what you could do. Your college professors expect much more. Just as you learned division and multiplication tables in elementary school and then went on to algebra in middle school, now you need more sophisticated ways to think about writing.

So, for the time being, forget the rules from your high school English classes—even AP English, if you took it. Forget about "thesis" and "conclusion." They'll still be there when you get back to them.

Let's try something different: Try looking at your essay the way a writer does instead of the way an English teacher does.

18. The Open House

Writing as Action

In high school most of us learned to think of essays objectively, as *things*. We produced W pages on X topic, with Y footnotes or citations and Z sources. The object, produced for our teacher's approval, contained certain required elements. The teacher graded it on how well it met the requirements and handed it back. We stashed it in a file somewhere, or on a computer drive, and promptly forgot about it.

As long as you keep that attitude in college, you'll tend to B.S. rather than be interesting. When you start off thinking of your essays as vessels to fill, you generally end up not much caring what you fill them with.

Traditional labels like *thesis* and *conclusion* and *body* often encourage you to ask yourself the wrong questions—questions such as: *Where do I put my thesis? Do I just restate my thesis in my conclusion? What goes in between?* Such questions encourage you to think of your essay as a collection of *things*. Instead of doing something, your essay tends to *be* something.

Good essays *do* things. When experienced writers sit down in front of their keyboards, they may not know exactly what they're going to say, but they aim to make stuff happen. Here are just a few examples of what essays can do:

| *Interpret* | *Report* | *Entertain* | *Reveal* |
| *Discover* | *Persuade* | *Evaluate* | *Explore* |

A good essay's organization and logical structure moves the reader from Point A (not knowing) to Point B (knowing). When you start thinking of your own essays that way, you've started to think like a writer.

Your House of Ideas

Home for you may mean Omaha, or Sacramento, or Washington, D.C., but for your ideas, home means … your head. That's where they live. When readers explore something you've written, you might say that they're coming to visit your ideas at home (Figure 18.1).

For the sake of this guide, let's picture your head as a vast, rambling mansion with millions of rooms, doors, and closets, linked by hallways, stairways, and maybe even a secret passage or two. You keep all sorts of stuff in those rooms—every fact you've ever learned, every brilliant deduction, every

IV: Writing the College Essay

Figure 18.1. Your House of Ideas

wacky theory, every instinctive connection, every unanswered question and half-formed intention. You're constantly adding new rooms to the place as you learn new stuff. Frankly, it's a mess.

When you write, you're essentially inviting a reader to come into the house, have a look around, and decide if she wants to "buy" your ideas.

That would be fine except for one problem—there's so much stuff packed in the rooms of your house, and so many rooms, that anyone besides you will get hopelessly lost. An essay offers you the chance to design a smaller version of the house where your ideas live, with carefully selected intellectual furnishings. Instead of millions and millions of rooms, it might have eight or ten, arranged in a logical, easy-to-navigate plan.

No "B.S." About

Structuring Your Essay

You want your readers to explore your ideas as if they were exploring a real estate "open house." Entice them to cross the threshold, show them

18. The Open House

around, and give them something to take away when they go. If you've written well, they'll "buy" the house and add it to their own mental architecture.

1. **Entice the Reader Across the "Threshold"**

    If you held an open house to attract prospective buyers, you'd try to make your house seem inviting by putting up signs on the street, flying balloons, and placing ads in your local newspaper. You'd also trim all the shrubs, mow the lawn, sweep up leaves and grass clippings, and put fresh flowers in the window-boxes. The whole idea would be to increase your house's "curb appeal," and convince prospective buyers to come inside and look around.

    The opening of a good essay does much the same thing. Its title and opening paragraphs challenge or invite readers into the intellectual structure. You catch your readers' attention, interest them in what's inside, and get them to cross the threshold into the argument itself.

2. **Sell Your Premise with an "Agent"**

    Just as a real-estate agent waits inside an open house, and talks to potential buyers who stop by to look around, the "agent" of your essay engages curious readers and encourages them to "buy" your idea. This part of an essay, like a traditional *thesis*, suggests the premise of your argument, and where you're going with it, much as a real-estate agent might point out the number of bedrooms and bathrooms, the hardwood floors, the well-equipped kitchen, and the walk-in closets of a house.

    So, why not just call it a *thesis*? Because the thesis has traditionally been defined as a kind of proposition—literally a "placing" (from the Latin *tithenai*, "to place") of the main idea in an essay. Thinking about where to place the proposition in that way tends to turn your idea into something static, rather than making it work and do things. Unlike a thesis, an agent *acts*. That's what your essay should do, too.

3. **Structure Your Essay According to a Clear "Plan"**

    The heart of any essay is its plan—the structure by which it organizes ideas. Using our "open house" metaphor, we might envision a *floor plan* that readers tour: the bedrooms, family rooms, bathroom, kitchen, and so forth. Do they have to cross the laundry room to get from the kitchen to the dining room? Are the bedrooms crowded next to the living room, where it's noisy? Is the kitchen too small? The plan determines the feel of the house—whether it seems inviting or claustrophobic—and finally

IV: Writing the College Essay

determines whether visitors can envision themselves "living there." The same will be true of your essay's plan.

Which plan you use for your essay will depend on what it's supposed to do. Does it compare things? Does it take a subject apart to see how it is constructed? Does it explain how something works? Does it argue for an interpretation? Here's where a writer can follow some proven designs so that one idea leads logically to the next. You can even combine various plans in a single paper. But if the overall plan doesn't make sense, your readers won't buy your ideas.

4. Conclude Your Essay with a Strong "Takeaway"

The last thing you say often has the biggest impact, as we saw in Part II. So, just as the last item in a list should be the most emphatic, you want the end of your essay to drive home your point memorably.

Typically, writing instructors have recommended that the "conclusion" of your essay sum up your argument, or re-state your thesis. But, if you read essays written by really good writers, that's rarely how they end. A *conclusion* means a final stop (the word literally means shutting down) to your argument. That's not really what you want your essay to do—you want it to keep going. You want the ideas you've explored to stay with the person who reads them so that they'll keep working, keep being thought about, and have a life beyond the dot at the end of your last sentence.

Instead of a conclusion, try thinking of the end of your essay as a *takeaway*—the part of your idea that you most want readers to take away[1] with them. Perhaps you'll do this through a memorable image, or a striking turn of phrase, or an amplification of what's come before: there are many good ways to wrap up an essay. As long as you think of it as something your readers can take away with them, you're moving in the right direction.

---

1. The biologist Richard Dawkins has proposed that we think of ideas passing from one person to another much in the way that genetic information passes from one organism to another during reproduction. Instead of a gene, Dawkins has invented the term meme to describe how ideas propagate themselves. Similarly, the Internet has led to phenomena called viral videos and viral marketing, where memes spread like a virus through social networks. The "takeaway" from your essay may not be as virulent as a video, but interesting ideas, like laughter, can be infectious too.

19

Introduction and Threshold

Most people are reluctant to walk out on a speech, but a reader can simply stop reading. — Walter Beale

So, where to start?

How do you get the reader to open the door to your house of ideas? Every writer faces that question with every new paper, report, letter, story, memo, or poem. Most high school writing courses teach you to start a paper with your thesis.

Right. Here goes:

This paper will demonstrate that the world is not flat.

Hmm. Bor-*ing*. How about:

Throughout history, mankind has mostly thought that the world was round.

Not much better. Let's see…

Round. Like a ball. That was the world.

Arrgh! (Sound of paper crumpling and bathroom door slamming.)

Okay, you already know that your introduction is important. But that just increases the pressure: how do you sum up all your research, thinking, worrying, and brainstorming into a few lines? It's no wonder that most college paper introductions end up sounding like they were written by Siri or Alexa or the voice on your phone's answering system.

This chapter offers a few suggestions that may make it easier, as you'll see below. But, before you go there, consider what an introduction should do.

What Your Reader Wants to Know

If you ever take a course in journalism, you'll learn that you start each news story with the most important thing, then include everything else—in

IV: Writing the College Essay

descending order of importance, or interest.[1] That's because journalists understand that their readers usually just want to know one thing: "What happened?" They also know that no one has to read a newspaper, a website, or a blog. If the story isn't interesting, or important, the reader will turn the page or click on a link to the latest basketball scores and news about Beyoncé and Kim Kardashian.

Unfortunately, journalistic writing doesn't work for most college essays. Your professor probably wants to learn more than just "what happened?" She wants to see that you've entered the academic conversation, evaluate what you know and how you reason, and hear what you've got to say.

As described in the previous chapter, the beginning of the paper gets the conversation started—it brings your reader with you to the "threshold" of the topic in an interesting way. Once the reader crosses that threshold, and enters the house with you, everything will depend on how well you argue your essay. But none of that will matter if you don't get the reader interested in the first place.

Bringing Your Reader In

Your introduction should do four things:

1. "Attract your reader's attention and focus it on the subject."[2]
2. "Provide necessary background information for a particular audience"—identifying "the general problem that the paper addresses as well as the particular issues" at hand.
    Is the issue one spurred by current events?
    Is it a matter of scholarly debate?
    Is it a matter of overlooked history?
3. "Clearly signal your own point of view or the direction of your argument."
    In a short essay this usually means a statement of your thesis (or "agent")

---

1. This is known among journalists as the "inverted pyramid" (♦) structure. In journalism, where most writing occurs under very tight deadlines, this structure has several advantages: It provides a kind of automatic road-map for writers. It gets readers to the point quickly. It allows editors to shorten stories by cutting them from the bottom up. And, it has the added advantage of keeping reporters from worrying too much about turning their lead (or "lede") paragraph into a work of art.

2. The quotations from this section are taken from Walter Beale, *Real Writing*.

19. Introduction and Threshold

4. "Establish ... the image of yourself that you wish to project" to the reader, and what "special relationship" you have to the subject or audience.
   Are you a guide? An advocate? An investigator?
   Does this topic affect you personally?
   Do you have personal experience that's relevant?[3]

Sometimes, if you're lucky (or good), you can perform several of these tasks simultaneously, in a sentence or two. Obviously, that's a lot to fit into one paragraph, much less one sentence. Usually you end up stressing one or two of them at the expense of others. If you're writing a paper of more than a couple of pages, you have room to develop your introduction. In a long essay or research paper (say, 15 pages or so), you can safely spin your introduction out over a page or more.

As a rule, the more your reader knows about your subject, the less you have to say to bring him to the threshold of the argument. So, for instance, if you're writing about a controversy that's all over the news, you may not have to explain much. If you're writing a paper about *Sense and Sensibility* for a professor who's a Jane Austen expert, a lengthy plot summary may not be necessary. Or, if your main point has a lot of natural drama to it, you can simply announce the topic, and charge into the paper.

For most academic topics, though, you're dealing with interpretations and subtleties, so you need to provide background and context without boring your reader. Unlike most writing outside of college, where your reader can simply quit if you bore him, academic etiquette demands that your professor read what you've written. But even so, a boring or clumsy introduction usually means an dissatisfied professor—and a lower grade.

Reaching the Threshold

Remember, the intro just gets things rolling.

Don't strain to pack your whole paper into the introduction. Just be relevant, and aim at bringing your reader to the argumentative threshold in a thoughtful, or challenging, or even funny way.

So how do you tell when you've gotten your reader to the "threshold"

---

3. The author gratefully acknowledges Walter Beale of the University of North Carolina at Greensboro for granting permission adapt a portion of his book *Real Writing* in this chapter.

of an argument? There's no infallible rule, but it's the point at which you've adequately prepared your reader to grapple with your ideas about your topic. By the time you get there she should be interested, she should recognize certain important issues, she should understand why you're involved, and she should be ready to hear you out. That's the point at which you need to point her in the right direction by offering the argument's "agent" (or thesis), as the next chapter will describe.

Begin in the Middle

Having introduction troubles? Try beginning in the middle!

In a famous bit of advice from Lewis Carroll's *Alice's Adventures in Wonderland*, the King tells Alice to

> Begin at the beginning. Continue on until you get to the end. Then stop.

Like most everything else in *Alice*, it's deliberate nonsense. Here's a dirty little secret: good writers often *begin in the middle*.

What does that mean for you? It may mean plunging right into the main argument of your paper. Even before you've written anything (if you've done the required research) you'll know the general focus of your topic and the main points you want to explore. Go ahead—start exploring! As you write the middle paragraphs, following your "plan" (Ch. 21), you'll often begin to better understand what you really want to focus on, and what your conclusion will be. Once you know that, you're ready to go back and write the introduction.

One word of caution, though. Don't just write the paper and then sticky-note an introduction and thesis on top of it. The paper should flow naturally out of the introduction. After you've drafted the introduction, go back through the whole paper and rework it from beginning to end so that the body and conclusion proceed smoothly and logically from the introduction. Or, as the King in *Alice* probably should have said, if he'd been offering sensible advice for writers:

- *Begin in the middle.*
- *Continue on until you get to the end.*
- *Then introduce it.*
- *When you've finished the introduction, rewrite everything so that it flows naturally from the introduction.*
- *Then stop.*

19. Introduction and Threshold

No "B.S." About

Introduction Strategies

You can start an essay in many ways, but here are some tried-and-true models that Walter Beale[4] has identified:

1. **Thesis Opening.** Concentrate attention by "stating your thesis right at the beginning ... in a bold and provocative way." This works especially well for arguments about current, controversial issues or when you're taking a contrarian approach. It's also a good technique for essay exams, where you can't spend a lot of time worrying about your introduction:

   > The stereotyped picture of medieval authorities who believed in a "flat earth" comes from the superstitions of sailors, not the writings of philosophers from that time. Most people who'd studied the subject had figured out that the world was round.

2. **Rebuttal.** Like the thesis opening, the rebuttal strategy gets right to the point. But it "comes out swinging." Typically, you disagree with another point of view, "sometimes a more popular one," and "clarify or draw attention to your own point of view" through the contrast:

   > To a Muslim, [Matt Yglesias argues,] something that's "jihad" is by definition a good thing, so when US officials refer to adversaries as "jihadists" we're implicitly accepting their definition of the conflict as one pitting Muslim holy warriors against enemies of the faith.... Matt is suggesting this is a bad thing, but I'd disagree. We called Nazis "Nazis" and we called communists "communists," and those were both things those groups called themselves. We didn't feel like we had to make up some weird, portmanteau name like "Islamofascist" because otherwise we'd be tacitly accepting the worldview of our enemies.—Kevin Drum, The Washington Monthly

3. **Problem or Controversy.** "The strategy here is to present (or recall) an important problem or controversy. The essay will either explain something about the problem or suggest solutions":

   > Two political scientists found that young people who watch Jon Stewart's faux news program, "The Daily Show," develop cynical views about politics

---

4. Real Writing.

IV: Writing the College Essay

and politicians that could lead them to just say no to voting.—Richard Morin, *The Washington Post*

4. **Focusing Event.** Start by presenting (or recalling) "a particular situation or set of circumstances. The essay either addresses the event head-on, as a problem in itself, or indirectly, as something symptomatic of a larger problem":

> In what is being touted as the biggest event of its kind in 30 years, an Antarctic ice shelf has collapsed and broken up into thousands of icebergs, the US-based National Snow and Ice Data Center reported. On its website, the center said a major part of the Larsen B ice shelf, believed to have been there for up to 12,000 years, had collapsed over a 35-day period.—Agence France-Presse

5. **Analogy or Parallel Case.** "The strategy here is to begin with the description or presentation of a situation ... analogous or parallel to the one you are writing about. Analogy can be particularly effective when ... [criticizing] some act or development":

> We are on patrol today in Iraq. Men and women of the United States armed forces in armored vehicles patrol the streets of Baghdad. They pass in the way of so many who have come before them: the Egyptian charioteers of Ramses II, the Macedonian phalanx of Alexander the Great, the Roman legionnaires of Caesar and Trajan, the Crusaders of Richard the Lion-Hearted, the legionnaires of Napoleon, the Camel Corps of Lawrence of Arabia.
> All of these have come through the Middle East. Many of them have come with the best of intentions, by their lights, to bring stability, even freedom to the Middle East. All have passed away. The Middle East has been the graveyard of empires.—J. Rufus Fears, The Heritage Foundation Lecture

6. **focusing quotation.** "This opener uses a quotation as a kind of focusing event. Where do you get quotations? You either (1) remember them; (2) get them from any reading or research you have been doing on your subject; or (3) look them up" on the Web or in a book of quotations:

> Mark Twain once wrote, "When you catch an adjective, kill it. No, I don't mean utterly, but kill most of them—then the rest will be valuable." Twain's ideas about prose style still guide the best of today's writers.

7. **focusing question.** Pose an interesting question. "Your thesis will generally be the answer to the question":

> Was the modernist poet Ezra Pound really anti–Semitic? Or was it all just a literary pose?

19. Introduction and Threshold

8. **confession or personal introduction.** "Sometimes the situation is right for this. Your subject concerns you in such a personal way that your best strategy is to explain your own involvement in it":

> As a young newspaper reporter, my editors taught me that the facts don't lie, and reporting them accurately was the mark of a professional. By that standard, what should I make of Jack Burden, the cynical journalist/political operative who narrates Robert Penn Warren's novel, *All the King's Men*?

Avoid tired, cookie-cutter introductions. Just as there are some tried and true ways to start a paper, there are also some too-often-tried and truly dull ways that virtually guarantee an eye-rolling response from your reader. Here, then, are some introductions to avoid:

> **The creaky, mechanical opener.** "The purpose of this essay is to…" "The thesis of this essay is…"
> **The grandiose opener.** "All through the ages mankind has sought to…"
> **The cliché opener.** "In today's modern world…"[5]
> **The dramatic "soap opera" opener.** "Thump … thump … there was a noise on the front porch…" [Beale].

---

5. If you ever find yourself writing something like, "Throughout history …" or "Across all the world …" get up and splash some cold water in your face. After all, have you studied all of history? Do you know everything that has happened since the beginning of time? Are you familiar with all the habits of African Bushmen? No? Maybe, then, you're crossing the B.S. threshold. Big, sweeping generalizations like those are the mark of someone who's just using prefabricated phrases and hasn't really thought the thing through. A more exact phrase—one that you can actually defend, if challenged—makes you sound like you know what you're talking about.

20

Agent and Thesis

The world is round; it has no point.—Adrienne Gusoff

Once you've gotten your reader interested, and brought him to the threshold of the essay's argument, it's time to start getting to the point. (Your reader expects you to have a point, so you'd better not disappoint him.)

This has traditionally been the job performed by an essay's *thesis*—something you've probably been taught ever since you wrote your first paper, years ago. It was solid advice. Your thesis is, very simply, your main point—the beating heart of your essay. It gives your essay life and purpose. Without it, your essay will die, bleeding away into pointlessness.

But there are a lot of misconceptions out there about the role that a thesis plays in an essay. So, what is a thesis? What does it do?

- It's not the same thing as your conclusion (*although it can be*).
- It's not merely a kind of "topic sentence" for your essay (*although a sentence like that might be a good idea when you're writing a timed essay exam, or short paper*).
- It doesn't have to sit at the end of the first paragraph or introduction (*although that's often where you'll put it*).
- It doesn't always have to be explicitly stated (*although it's frequently wise to explicitly state it*).

As you can see, there's more than one way to construct a thesis. Remember, writing is an *art* (about *doing* things) rather than a *science* (about *knowing* things); how you do it depends on what you're doing.

You were probably taught otherwise. Just as your middle school science teacher might have taught you to remember the visual spectrum of light by introducing you to Mr. "Roy G. Biv" (Red, Orange, Yellow, Green, Blue, Indigo, Violet), your English teachers gave you firm rules about writing a thesis to drill the concept of *having* a thesis into your head. Now that you're

20. *Agent and Thesis*

in college, though, you're past the basics, and you're ready to start writing some of the other colors of the spectrum.

This really shouldn't come as a surprise. Think about the most interesting essays and stories that you've ever read: has the writer always come out and planted a big sign saying, in effect, "HERE BE YE THESIS" or "THIS IS MY MEANING"? It's pretty rare. Sometimes, as a reader, that's frustrating—you *want* writers to tell you exactly what they mean. But maybe the writer wants you to be engaged, rather than passively consume—he wants you to figure out the meaning yourself, rather than just have conclusions handed to you on a plate.

In some excellent essays it's hard to find a clearly stated thesis at all. That doesn't mean there's no thesis there. Certain kinds of essays require an explicitly stated thesis. Others don't.

So, how do you tell which is which? By understanding who your reader is. If your reader has asked you a direct question—the way a professor does on an essay exam question—he expects a direct answer. If you're inviting your reader to think about the complexities of an issue—as you might if your professor has assigned an open-ended paper—perhaps something more indirect will work better.

Okay, you say. That's fine. But what am I supposed to do when I try to write an essay if I'm not sure where to put my thesis? Good question. It might help to think of your thesis in another way—as an *agent*.

The Pitch

Let's go back to our metaphor of an "open house," from Chapter 18. Your introduction has gotten the reader interested, and brought him up to the threshold of your "house of ideas." Now's the time for the agent to go to work.

When a real-estate agent holds an open house, she typically waits near a home's front door and greets potential buyers as they poke their heads inside. Her job, at that point, is to make a pitch. Typically, she does it by telling them some things about the house:

> This historic three-bedroom house was once home to our town's mayor. You'll find that the current owners have refurbished the kitchen with all-new appliances, and added a laundry room. There's a big back yard for your kids, and a nice screened-in porch that would be great for summer cookouts. The owners have just reduced their price, and homes in this neighborhood have been steadily increasing in value over the last decade.

Why does the agent do this? Why not just let visitors explore it on their own? Because, by pointing out the features of the house, and telling visitors what they can expect to find, she directs their exploration and helps them see what she wants them to see. By casting the house as "historic," rather than "old," she prepares them to think well of its old-fashioned features and to see its possibilities. By stressing the renovations and additions, she makes it seem like a living, evolving place. By mentioning the back yard and screened porch, she helps the visitors envision themselves relaxing there. By mentioning the price and neighborhood, she helps them see the house as a good investment.

In other words, the agent's job is to offer context and direction. If she does her job well, she allows visitors to appreciate the house as they tour it, discovering things that reinforce what she's suggested. If she does her job badly (say, by exaggerating or misleading them about what they'll see, or by not having useful information), they will be disappointed by what they find and ill-disposed to investigate further. Different agents have different styles. Some come on with a hard sell, with floor-plans and photos and market values, and follow visitors around as they tour. Some offer cookies and coffee and small talk, hint at a few things the visitors might find, and let them explore at their leisure. There's no single way to do it.

In your essay, the agency statement does much the same thing. It suggests a structure for the reader to follow as he explores your ideas. It may ask questions that the essay will answer. It may point to where the essay is going, and show how it's going to get there. It may mention what the reader will encounter along the way, and it may leave certain things for the reader to discover on his own.

The Agent in Your Essay

As we've said, good writers think of their essays as *doing* things—explaining, exploring, arguing, discovering, motivating, and so forth. The agent, whether a classic "thesis statement" or not, propels the essay forward as an action, and gives your reader a context for thinking about what you've said.

Your essay's agent need not be a long sales pitch. It can be a sentence or two at the beginning, or a paragraph near the end of an introduction. It can pose a question that the essay will explore and that the conclusion will answer. It can make a claim that the rest of the essay will defend. It can be something

20. Agent and Thesis

that the essay keeps coming back to and reviewing, as it moves through the evidence.

Here are excerpts from four famous arguments. Let's see how the "agent" differs from the "thesis" in each, and what they have in common.

1. When in the Course of human events it becomes necessary for one people to dissolve the political bands which have connected them with another and to assume among the powers of the earth, the separate and equal station to which the Laws of Nature and of Nature's God entitle them, a decent respect to the opinions of mankind requires that they should declare the causes which impel them to the separation.—The Declaration of Independence
2. [Our use of language] becomes ugly and inaccurate because our thoughts are foolish, but the slovenliness of our language makes it easier for us to have foolish thoughts. The point is that the process is reversible.—George Orwell, "Politics and the English Language"
3. Must the citizen ever for a moment, or in the least degree, resign his conscience to the legislator?—Henry David Thoreau, "Civil Disobedience"
4. In a sense we have come to our nation's capital to cash a check.—Martin Luther King, "I Have a Dream"

Agent 1 is pretty straightforward. It says, essentially, that when people declare political independence, they'd better be able to explain themselves and provide some reasons. Since the Declaration is essentially a long list of reasons why the American colonies have been badly treated by the British Empire, it's a provocative way to start. From reading that agency statement, the first sentence of the Declaration, we expect to hear good reasons described and explained to us. The thesis develops out of the many examples that follow: that people subjected to political tyranny have the right to free themselves. The agent at the beginning implies it, but doesn't specifically spell it out.

Agent 2 is probably the closest of these four examples to a "traditional" thesis. It comes after an introduction, in the essay's second paragraph. Orwell proposes that poorly used language can cause us to make bad political decisions, and that improving the way we use language can improve our political IQ. He then spends the rest of the essay illustrating what he means—showing examples of bad language, showing how government uses language to hide things, and showing how an intelligent command of language can remedy some of the habits of mind that make bad government possible.

IV: Writing the College Essay

Agent 3 asks a question that drives Thoreau's essay forward. He asks it in the third paragraph of his essay. As readers, we want to learn the answer, so we keep reading. Thoreau's ultimate answer—"No!"—forms his thesis, but rather than just coming out and stating it plainly, he uses the agent of the question to lead us into a lengthy exploration of issues of personal responsibility, patriotism, and justice. After he's explored the theory and logic of his position, he offers an extended concrete example—a story about why he went to jail one day rather than pay taxes that he considered unjust. The question, rather than the thesis, is what keeps us interested, and moving forward through the essay.

Agent 4 uses a metaphor to move the argument forward. King's thesis is that America has broken its promises to black people, something he doesn't say explicitly until the middle of the speech. His agent, in the second paragraph of his speech, gets us to think about the whole question of promises: a check is a promise to pay money, and what black people have brought to Washington, D.C., on the day of his speech is a "bounced" check. They're demanding payment—demanding that a promise be kept. That metaphor propels us into the speech to see how the "story" of the bad check will end. And, of course, the story ends with King's famous inspirational vision about an America of promises kept, fairness, equality, and social justice.

In each of these examples, the agent engages the reader and signals where the argument will go. And, along the way to completing that action through the larger essay or speech, the writer conveys a thesis.

Keeping Promises

Another way to look at the agent is as a kind of bargain you make with your readers. After you've caught their interest, and brought them to the threshold of the argument, the agent makes a promise that the essay will fulfill. It may be to inform your readers, or to answer a question, or to survey a number of related issues, or to complete some other kind of action. The point is, with that implied promise in mind, your readers will be more open to hearing what you have to say.

When you write the conclusion, or "takeaway" of your essay (Chapter 22), be sure to look back to your agent. If it has posed a question, or set forth a challenge, decide whether the body of your essay has satisfied the expectation you've raised. If not, you'll need to make sure that the takeaway addresses it. There's nothing more frustrating to readers than having an essay draw them in with a provocative question, only to leave the question hanging. Keep your promises.

No "B.S." About

Agent and Thesis

- **Your Thesis Is Your "Main Point"; Know What It Is.**

  If you can't tell yourself what the main point of your essay is, you've got big problems. After you've finished the essay, read it over again and ask yourself, "What's my main point." If the answer isn't clear, go back and revise.

- **Where You Put Your Thesis Depends on Your Audience.**

  In short papers and essay exams, do what your high-school teachers taught you: include a clearly stated thesis in the first paragraph, or near the beginning of the essay. Longer writing assignments offer more flexibility. For instance, your thesis could be in your conclusion, or could answer a question (the agent) that you've posed at the beginning of the essay. Or it could appear halfway through the essay, after you've clearly defined a problem. Or it could be implied, rather than explicitly stated. Take a careful look at the assignment and decide what kind of leeway it gives you.

- **Make Sure There's an Agent at the Threshold.**

  Every essay should have an agent—a statement, question, image, metaphor, or other device—that makes a promise to the reader early in the essay. The agent is particularly important if you're not stating your thesis right away. It may map out the argument of a long, complicated paper. It may hint at the answer and challenge the reader to watch you get there. It may show a problem to be solved. It may make a dramatic assertion that requires support. Whatever form your agent takes, it belongs at the point where you've hooked your reader and are launching into the body of your essay. Make sure your reader knows where you're going.

- **Think of Your Essay as Doing Something.**

  Don't make the mistake of simply filling up your essay with facts. Use the facts to *do* something. The agent starts that action.

IV: Writing the College Essay

- **Keep Your Promises.**

    The agent of your essay announces or implies a promise to the reader. But, to paraphrase the Amazing Spider-Man, with great promises come great responsibilities: make sure that when you reach the takeaway for your essay you keep whatever promises your agent makes at the threshold.

21

Plan

We never know how high we are
Till we are called to rise;
And then, if we are true to plan,
Our statures touch the skies.
—Emily Dickinson

Although it's crucial to get your reader to the argumentative threshold, and it's essential to have an agent that indicates what your essay will do, those won't amount to anything without taking the next step—presenting the facts, research, logical arguments, and stories that make up the body of your essay.

Inevitably you'll end up sweating most over beginnings and endings, but most of what you write will be this "body," which needs structure too. That's where a *plan* comes in. In this chapter, we'll review a smorgasbord of different plans for essays, and suggest ways that you can use them separately—and in combination—for your own writing.

What a Plan Does

An adventure novel carries the reader along by linking particular incidents into a long, eventful story, with the promise of an exciting conclusion. A traditional sonnet sets out a certain pattern of rhyme and meter, and structures a poetic message to fit it. A play connects scenes and acts set in different places and times to complete a dramatic action. All of these are "plans." College essays follow plans too.

Returning to the metaphor of an open house that we introduced in Chapter 16, remember that most homes have a certain logic to them—the great room is near the entryway, the bedrooms are near bathrooms, the kitchen is near the dining room, and so forth. Often the real estate agent will map out the house for visitors, describing the way that the rooms are laid out, where hallways lead,

IV: Writing the College Essay

where the walk-in closets are, and so forth (in an essay, this "map" belongs in the agency statement). Then she sends the visitors off to explore on their own. With that description in mind, visitors will explore the house from room to room until they have a good sense of how it's put together and of what it would be like living there. It helps to think of your essay in much the same way.

After your essay's agent has promised what the essay will do, the plan organizes how it does it.

For example, a typical exam question in a political philosophy course might be something like the following:

> Briefly compare the concept of the ideal state as it appears in Plato's *Republic* and Aristotle's *Politics*. Give examples and discuss.

Figure 21.1 shows a sample argumentative plan[1] that you might use for an essay question like that:

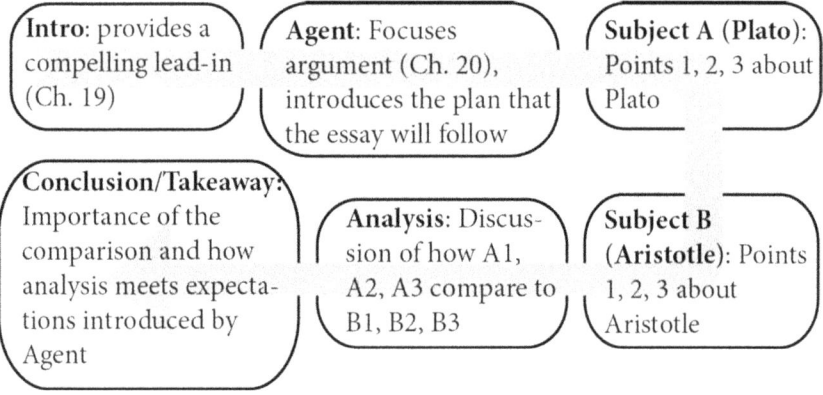

Figure 21.1. Sample plan: Comparison of two subjects

This plan uses the comparison and contrast model described in Section ii below. Other such short assignments might require you to analyze a text, compose a policy argument, develop a classification, or explain a process. Most of the plans in this chapter are well suited to short papers and essay exams.

---

1. Like an outline, a plan such as that in Figure 21.1 helps you visualize the shape of an essay. Formal outlines do much the same thing, but many writers actually find them inhibiting when they're drafting their essays. Your author prefers to actually draw out his plans, with boxes and arrows, so that the shape of an essay becomes apparent. You may find that a traditional outline works better for you.

21. Plan

In a house, you'd expect the floor plan to logically connect one room with the next. You don't expect to have to go through the bathroom to get from the kitchen to the dining room, for instance. In much the same way, the plan of your essay should allow the reader to move logically through your argument. How it does so depends on the type of essay you're writing. In the subsections that follow, we'll look at some model "houses" you can use.

Seven Basic Plans

There are dozens of different ways to plan an essay, but you'll find these seven particularly useful for the kinds of college writing assignments you typically encounter on exams, quizzes, and short papers. Deciding which plan to use will often depend on the wording of your professor's assignment.

I. **Narration and Description**—Describing a subject and telling a story about it.
   Sample assignment question: "Describe the political events in Congress leading up to Lincoln's decision to issue the Emancipation Proclamation."
II. **Comparison**—Exploring differences and similarities of subjects and ideas.
   Sample assignment question: "What are some key differences between the Keynesian and monetarist schools of economic theory? Compare and contrast."
III. **Process Analysis and Explanation**—Explaining how things happen, and in what order.
   Sample assignment question: "Outline the major steps followed in the process of gene sequencing."
IV. **Cause and Effect**—Finding causes and describing effects.
   Sample assignment question: "To what extent was the 1979 Iranian hostage crisis responsible for the "Reagan Revolution" of the 1980s? Describe and discuss."
V. **Division and Classification**—Dividing a single subject into several classes, or grouping scattered subjects into several classes.
   Sample assignment question: "What are the major sections of a symphony orchestra, and why are they divided in that way?"

IV: Writing the College Essay

VI. **Argumentation**—Making a case for or against an idea.
   Sample assignment question: "Argue for or against the proposal to lower the U.S. voting age to 16."

VII. **Definition**—Developing an argument about meaning.
   Sample assignment question: "Democratic Party candidates now prefer to be identified as 'progressive' rather than 'liberal'; what does *liberal* mean in today's political environment?"

Planning the Long Essay

Sometimes one of these plans can sustain a long paper just as it does a short essay. But what if you've been assigned a long research or analytical essay? It sometimes helps to come at the essay in several different ways, as in Figure 21.2, which examines Plato's ideal state in comparison with Aristotle's.

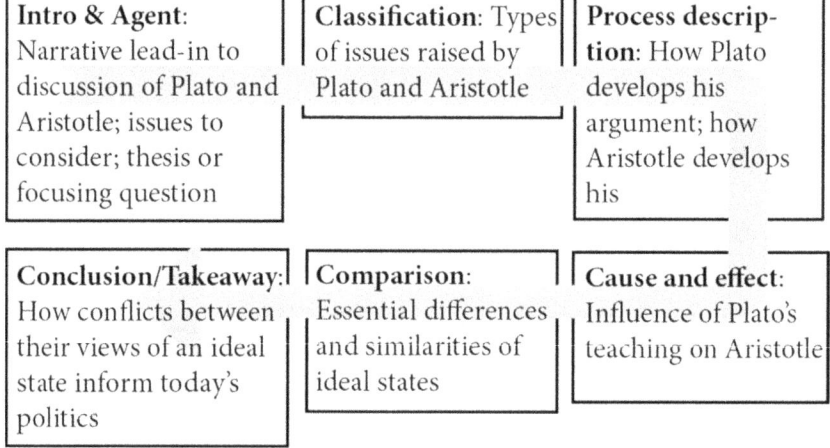

Figure 21.2. Combining Plans to Build a Longer Essay

With the prospect of writing fifteen pages facing you, a mixed plan like this helps make a big job more manageable. Each section becomes a kind of mini-essay, like chapters in a book, the topics linked by the larger essay's agent. Breaking your essay up into smaller parts also gives you more to say, and decreases the likelihood that you'll have to B.S. your way through to

21. Plan

meet a required page count or number of words. In fact, some of the plans—definition and argumentation in particular—*require* you to bring in comparisons, descriptions, and other elements in combination.

Let's look at them in detail.

I. Narration and Description

From national myths and religious scriptures to innocuous questions like "So, how was your day?" we depend on narration and description to help us construct meaning out of what's going on around us. Stories structure our lives, and they structure many a college essay as well.

What Happened?

There's a good reason journalists call their articles "stories." Most journalism tries to answer the classic "5W+H" questions that all reporters memorize: *Who? What? When? Where? Why?* and *How?* By answering those questions in the form of a story, a writer provides a natural structure that the reader can understand without having to wheel out heavy interpretive equipment.

Stories convey a lot of information in a hurry and usually mean that the storyteller has already filtered out things that aren't important. That's why a journalist who has been assigned to report on the latest federal economic statistics bulletin knows she won't get many readers by presenting a table of figures. Instead, she tries to convey the *stories* that the statistics tell: "Americans declared bankruptcy in record numbers," or "Service sector jobs are begging for people to fill them," or "New home-buyers find low adjustable mortgage-interest rates a mixed blessing."

Stories begin and end, with stuff occurring in between—they're like a time sandwich. We "bite" them because we instinctively want to know what happened so that we can decide what we should do next: Do we act? Are we okay? Should we plan? Should we worry?

In that respect, we're not really that different from our prehistoric ancestors who drew pictures on cave walls illustrating narratives that explained what they saw and experienced. Nor are we different from the first tellers of stories from ancient Greece. Many essays require you to provide a history of your subject, and the word history, in fact, derives from the Greek *historia*: "finding out, narrative." Stories remain the most accessible way to convey important information. When combined with accurate description, they remain an effective way to write many academic papers.

IV: Writing the College Essay

What Are the Details?

Here's where you put description to work. Take another look at Chapter 5 now. As we saw there, specific details offer data that we can "see," "hear," "taste," "touch," and "smell." They're the proof that a narrative conveys.

When you employ a narrative/descriptive strategy, it's not enough merely to tell the story:

> In the beginning, God created the heaven and the earth.—Genesis 1: 1

You also have to provide details that make the story believable:

> But there went up a mist from the earth, and watered the whole face of the ground. And the Lord God formed man of the dust of the ground, and breathed into his nostrils the breath of life....—Genesis 2: 6–7

When you offer your reader a narrative exposition, don't make the mistake of merely providing abstract summary. Get specific. If, for instance, you're providing the factual background for a paper on Islamic religious practices, don't simply generalize and offer a vague statement like, "Islam requires Muslims to make a pilgrimage to Mecca." Flesh it out with details:

> Muslim pilgrims travel to Saudi Arabia and are transported to hotels and "tent cities" catering to the week-long Hajj. From those camps, they embark by the millions to perform symbolic rituals in the cities of Mecca and Medina, visiting the tomb of the Prophet Mohammed, circling three times around the ancient cube-shaped building known as the Ka'baa, racing back and forth across the Great Mosque to reenact Ishmael and Hagar's search for water, and throwing stones at pillars in the desert that represent *Shaitan* (an evil *jinn*, or spirit, known in other religions as Satan).

Description also means describing ideas, not just facts. Often, when introducing a concept in a narrative, you'll need to describe the concept using examples and explanations of specific terms. You can describe an idea, such as *photosynthesis*, as readily as you can describe a thing, such as *carbon dioxide*.

What Have We Seen?

With narrative/descriptive papers, you have two basic organizational options:

1. Discuss the details as you go (Figure 21.3, integrated discussion).
2. Discuss the details in a separate section (Figure 21.4, analytical discussion).

21. Plan

Many narrative essays like those you'll encounter in magazines tend to follow the model of Figure 21.3. The writer gives the story primary focus, while the discussion of what the narrative and descriptions mean or teach often appears elliptically in comments and throwaway lines, as the writer tells the tale. As the story progresses and the details accumulate, the meaning becomes clear.

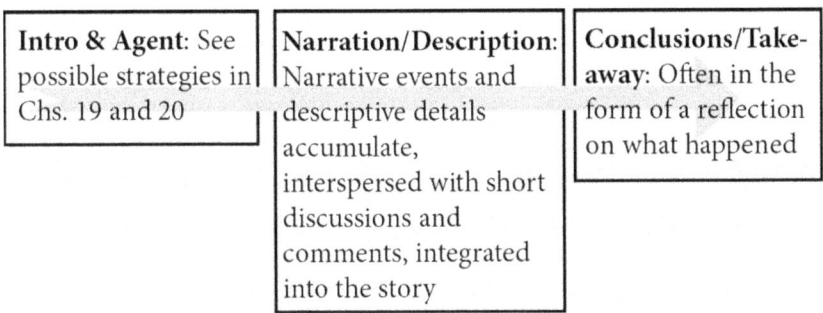

Figure 21.3. Narrative Essay Structures: Integrated Discussion

Academic narrative essays tend to be more like the model shown in Figure 21.4. The writer tells a story and provides details that offer data, then steps back and discusses the "meaning"—what the narrative and details have shown. This model resembles that of the "Basic Analytical Paragraph" of Chapter 11.

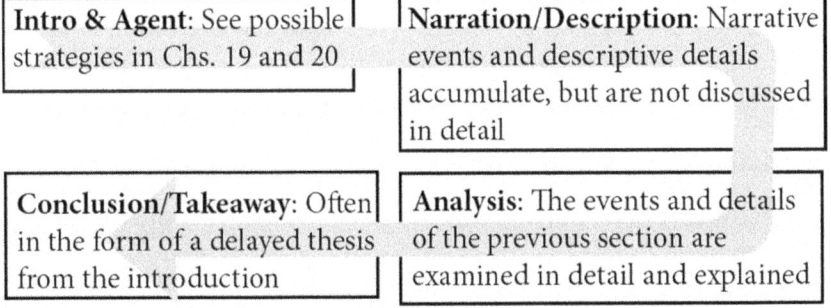

Figure 21.4. Narrative Essay Structures: Analytical Discussion

Narration and description become crucial when you use the argumentation plan (Section vi below). In fact, as Chapter 12 discussed, the classical structure of an argument includes a *narration* section, where the writer lays out the problem to be argued about. It's something that writers and orators have done ever since the time of the ancient Greeks, so don't write it off as mere "storytelling." It's a vital part of college essays.

II. Comparison

College teaches critical thinking, and inevitably critical thinking means weighing one idea or thing against another. It's hard to know what's good if you don't know what's bad, after all. And we often define something in comparison with something else: We understand Aristotle better by comparing him to Plato.

That's where a comparison plan comes in. By examining similarities and differences, you see each subject more clearly and in a broader context. This might be the most useful of all the plans in this guide—a basic structure that you'll apply in many college essays and essay exam assignments.

A quick note about terminology: Many essay assignments will ask you to "compare and contrast" two or more subjects. This is actually a little redundant (whether you point this out to your professor or not is a risk you'll just have to weigh on your own). *Contrast* means seeing how things *differ*. *Comparison* means that too, but it also means to see how things *resemble* each other. When you see the "comparison and contrast" phrase, it usually means your instructor wants to discuss similarities *and* differences, not just how the subjects are different.

Finally, it's possible to compare three, four, or more subjects—just more complicated. For the sake of simplicity, let's limit this discussion to essays that compare two subjects, but you should feel free to extend these examples.

Methods of Comparison

In college essays, you'll usually want to choose between three models of comparison:

1. Subject-to-subject comparison
2. Point-to-point comparison
3. Comparison of similarities and differences

The three plans are often interchangeable, but subject-to-subject comparison (Figure 21.5) works best for short papers and essay exams, where you only have time to compare a few major points. Point-to-point comparison (Figure 21.6) works best for longer essays and papers in which there may be many points to compare. Comparison of similarities and differences (Figure 21.7) can work well in either long or short essays. There are other variations.

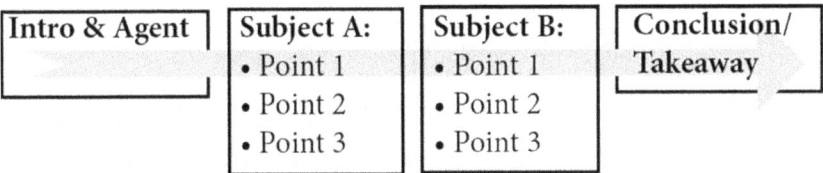

Figure 21.5. *Subject-to Subject Comparison (Comparison of Wholes)*

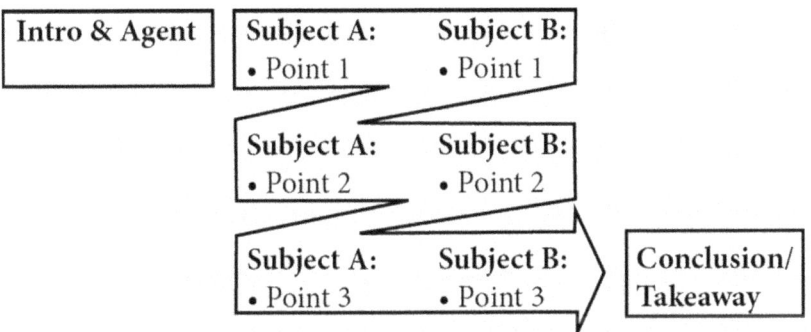

Figure 21.6. *Point-to-Point Comparison (Comparison of Parts)*

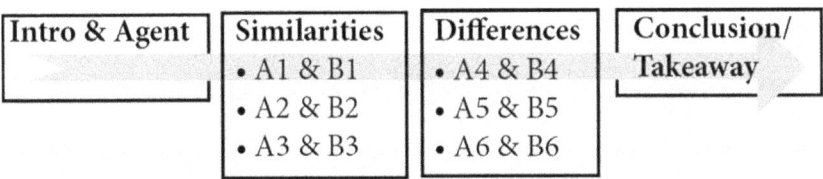

Figure 21.7. *Comparison of Similarities and Differences*

To illustrate how this works in practice, here's a brief prose outline of a short essay that uses Point-to-Point Comparison to compare two historic attacks on the United States. If your author were actually writing the essay, rather than just outlining it, he would flesh it out with narrative and descriptive examples, and discuss what the comparisons showed:

IV: Writing the College Essay

Agent: The shock of the September 11, 2001, attacks was like the 1941 Pearl Harbor attack that brought the U.S. into World War II.
Point 1: (A) In 1941 we thought we were at peace.
(B) On September 11, 2001, there were no active U.S. military operations.
Point 2: (A) We considered ourselves neutral "good guys" in 1941 and thought no one would want to attack us.
(B) Having recently "won" the Cold War, and imposed peace in the former Yugoslavia in 1998, we saw ourselves as a benevolent power in 2001.
Point 3: (A) Physical distance from Europe and Japan produced a false sense of security in 1941.
(B) Conflicts in the Middle East and Afghanistan seemed distant in 2001, since neither posed a nuclear threat.
Point 4: (A) In 1941, public opinion was focused inward, on U.S. problems left over from the Great Depression.
(B) In 2001, a recession and a recent controversial election led us to focus on internal politics and "culture wars."
Point 5: (A) Isolationist sentiments were strong in 1941.
(B) Similarly, in 2001 we were pulling out of international treaties and disengaging militarily in many places.
Takeaway: Mark Twain once said, "History does not repeat itself, but it rhymes." The September 11 attacks offer many "rhymes" with the Pearl Harbor attack. But the national reaction to the shock was quite different.

Note that all of the comparison models follow the rule of parallel construction discussed in Chapter 7: by following a predictable pattern, where a point about Subject A has its parallel in Subject B, you give your reader a kind of mental road map to follow. If you mixed up the comparisons and contrasts so that there wasn't any particular pattern to the order in which you presented them, your reader might spend more time wondering about what came next than on the comparisons you wanted her to think about.

III. Process Analysis and Explanation

Technology inflicts a lot of processes on us. Any time you open a computer manual, try to figure out how to operate the latest cell phone, or apply for a bank loan over the Internet, you rely on some writer to explain the

21. Plan

process clearly. Process analysis and explanation also have a big part to play in academic essays since much of what we do in college involves trying to understand how things work, or why things happened. You'll use this plan a lot.

The main difference between process explanation and process analysis has to do with the writer's purpose:

- Process explanation describes *how* something works.
- Process analysis investigates *why* something works the way it does.

Process Explanations—Lab reports in the sciences offer a straightforward example of process explanation. Your professor may ask you to describe the premise, process, and results of an experiment. What she wants from you is clear, objective description of the process, and straightforward presentation of the important data.

Here's a quick outline of a process explanation, from a science experiment:

Intro/Agent:
  In an experiment, groups of female mice were fed food with varying levels of pollen in it, to determine whether pollen content was related to the development of mammary tumors.

Plan (Steps):
  1. Control group and subject group were established.
  2. Pollen suspension prepared.
  3. Different mixtures of suspension prepared.
  4. Different groups of mice were fed the preparations for a specified period.
  5. Mice were weighed, amounts of food eaten recorded.
  6. Vaginal smears taken daily of mice in estrus.
  7. Samples examined microscopically for tumor cells

Takeaway:
  Results indicated development of mammary tumors in mice was delayed by ingestion of pollinated food.

Process Analysis—Sometimes, though, in order to explain how something works, you have to first take it apart and figure out why it works that way. That's where process analysis comes in. Remember that *analysis* means taking something apart (as opposed to synthesis, which means putting something together). Process analysis can be useful in sciences as well, as when you're analyzing the cause of an engineering failure, but it's particularly important in the humanities, when you're trying to analyze, for example, a series of historical events and show how they led to a particular outcome.

Intro/Agent:
Analysis showed that students who wrote "A" research papers in Dr. Rubin's composition class shared a common process in writing their papers.

Plan (Steps):
1. They conducted preliminary research on a topic that interested them to narrow it down to something arguable.
2. They consulted general reference sources (aside from Wikipedia) to get an overview of the topic.
3. They searched periodical indexes to get current popular and scholarly articles on the topic.
4. They found books that covered the topic in depth.
5. They carefully documented and paraphrased the sources, and picked appropriate quotations to illustrate important points.
6. They drafted the paper and got feedback from other students in the class.
7. They rewrote their drafts into a final version based on student feedback, and spent time improving the clarity and concision of their prose.

Takeaway:
The "A" papers were distinguished by their thorough research and their careful use of language. Typically, these papers were written by students who allowed sufficient time for research, drafting, and revision, and did not wait until the last minute.

IV. Cause and Effect

Cause and effect papers may sometimes resemble process analysis papers in that they seek to identify why something happened, or what happened after something occurred. They may even break a topic down into steps to do so. But cause-and-effect thinking tends to be broader and more speculative than process analysis, and it takes the form of several different patterns.

Determining cause and effect can be complicated. Here are some patterns you may encounter:

21. Plan

- *One cause: many effects.* (HIV virus → political, medical, social changes)
- *One effect: different causes.* (Losing the game ← bad strategy, injuries, poor execution)
- *Immediate cause: effect.* (Foam hitting wing → Space shuttle disaster)
- *Remote cause: effect.* (Complacency about foam risks → Space shuttle disaster)
- *Primary cause: effect.* (Global oil demand → High gas prices)
- *Secondary cause: effect.* (Hurricane Katrina → High gas prices)
- *Causal chain.* (President Clinton has sex with intern → Scandal breaks → Gore avoids Clinton in campaign → Gore is judged on personality instead of record as Clinton's Vice President → Bush wins election.
- *Necessary conditions.* (Hurricane Katrina → Massive flooding in New Orleans if New Orleans is below sea level.)

Types of Cause/Effect Essays

Essays that describe effects—A focus on what happened after a causative event.

Intro/Thesis: Higher gas prices changed public attitudes toward driving.
Effects: Sales of small cars rose, big SUVs fell.
Ridership on public transportation increased.
Fewer "driving vacations" were planned.
Video rentals and movie attendance increased.
Takeaway: Some parts of the economy benefited from changed patterns, and others suffered from them.

Essays that find causes—A focus on what happened before an effect.

Intro/Thesis: Effect—More students enrolled in community colleges during the Great Recession.
Causes: Bad economy made jobs more competitive.
Fewer students could afford four-year colleges.
Companies sought employees with specific skills that community colleges taught.
C.C. faculty quality rose due to increased pool of qualified teachers.
Takeaway: At a time when many colleges saw their enrollment drop, bad economic conditions led to increased demand at community colleges.

IV: Writing the College Essay

V. Division and Classification

Among the most useful plans you can use for longer papers is division and classification. Many academic projects involve analyzing a topic by dividing it up and classifying those parts. What is *Wikipedia*, after all, but a mammoth exercise of division of all the world's knowledge into its constituent parts, and classifications of those parts into well-organized chunks of information?

Division and classification are both about grouping things into classes. They just come at it from different angles.

Division in this context means taking a whole subject (such as plans for college papers) and using a consistent principle to divide them into smaller groups (this chapter uses seven classes, of which this is the fifth).

Classification involves taking scattered information (such as random ideas about writing) and using a consistent principle to group it into classes (this book gathers it into twenty-four chapters) that make logical sense.

Your thesis or agent should say whether you're dividing, classifying or combining the two, and describe why. Your takeaway should ask the "so what?" question: what was the purpose of the division/classification, and what did it prove?

A famous essay built around the principle of division and classification is George Orwell's "Politics and the English Language," one of the best-known arguments for clear, direct writing. Let's look at how it is organized:

Intro/Agent: Orwell claims that modern habits of writing produce both bad writing and immoral effects.
Data: He cites several examples of bad writing.
Classification: He classifies the writing faults seen in the data into several categories, and explains why they're bad:
1. Dying metaphors
2. Operators/verbal false limbs
3. Pretentious diction
4. Meaningless words

Argument: He argues that the problem in each case is that words are divorced from their meanings. This is expressed as a logical proposition:
- Each intends to hide meaning, not communicate it.
- Such bad writing can thus hide immoral actions.
- Therefore, bad writing encourages immoral action

Takeaway: Orwell argues that by writing well, and criticizing bad writing, we can combat immoral actions.

21. Plan

VI. Argumentation

Reread and reexamine Chapter 12, "Classical Argumentation", which outlines the basic structure that most arguments have followed for more than 2,000 years. It's one of the seven basic plans. We won't review it here, but instead will talk about another way of arguing, called *Rogerian Argument*.

Not all academic arguments aim at destroying the other side's position. Rogerian argument (named after psychologist Carl Rogers) seeks to bridge the gap between competing ideas, and is an alternative to the classical structure that seeks to defeat the other side's argument.

There are four elements to a Rogerian argument:

1. *Introduction and demonstration*—Describes the problem and demonstrates that you understand your opponent's position.
2. *Contextual statement*—Shows the contexts in which your opponent's ideas may make sense.
3. *Position statement*—Describes your position, and contexts in which it makes sense.
4. *Benefits statement*—Argues how your opponent's position would actually benefit from elements of your position.

Here's how you might use a Rogerian argument in the classical argumentative structure:

Introduction/Agent—Introduce the subject and reach the threshold where an agent statement shows that you understand the opposing view, but have a differing argument.

Refutation/Concession—Offer a Rogerian contextual statement that shows ways in which the opposing argument makes sense.

Confirmation—Offer a Rogerian position statement that shows the contexts in which your own view makes sense.

Conclusion/Takeaway—Focus on the benefits of your position to your opponent, and show how the ways in which the positions complement each other actually create a better solution than either single view.

VII. Definition

Quick: what's the difference between "bias," "prejudice," and "bigotry?"

The answer, actually, would make a good essay. Many such questions become topics for college essays that employ the strategy of *definition* as their

IV: Writing the College Essay

main organizing principle. And many other kinds of essays often need a definition section to limit and clarify their subjects.

Definition means more than just consulting a dictionary. The dictionary can be a good place to start, but remember that your professor usually wants to see *you* think; that means going a little farther—maybe even *arguing* with the dictionary definition or proposing an alternative. For example, asked for an oral report defining "pilgrimage" for a course on that subject, a student simply offered the following dictionary definition that she found on the Internet:

> **pil·grim·age** (pĭl′grə-mĭj) n.: 1. A journey to a sacred place or shrine. 2. A long journey or search, especially one of exalted purpose or moral significance. intr.v.: pil·grim·aged, pil·grim·ag·ing, pil·grim·ag·es. To go on a pilgrimage.[2]

Okay. As far as it goes. But what about a trip to visit Elvis's home at Graceland? Does that count? Or a six-month "thru-hike" on the Appalachian Trail? What makes something sacred? When a politician journeys to hold a highly publicized photo-op at "Ground Zero" in New York City, is that a pilgrimage? Or what about a writer who spends a year observing nature along a creek in the mountains of Virginia? And how about a Mississippi tour of stately homes called the "Natchez Pilgrimage?" All of those are examples that the student could have used to argue for a more thoughtful definition and that would have made her presentation more interesting.

Remember: somebody had to write that dictionary definition. It wasn't inscribed by divine fire on Mt. Zion. Maybe you can write a better definition to suit your purposes. Maybe arguing in favor of your definition would make a good essay.

Kinds of Definitions

Definitions come in many shapes and sizes, and perform different tasks in different kinds of essays. Here's a brief rundown of various kinds of definitions and some functions they perform.

Negative Definition—Often you can dramatically and effectively highlight what something is by starting with what it isn't:

> [L]ove is … not jealous, love does not boast, it is not inflated. It is not discourteous, it is not selfish, it is not irritable, it does not enumerate the evil. It does not rejoice over the wrong, but rejoices in the truth…—I Corinthians 13

---

2. "pilgrimage." *The American Heritage Dictionary of the English Language*, Fourth Edition (Boston: Houghton Mifflin Company, 2004).

21. Plan

As you can see, negative definition has an ancient and distinguished pedigree. But it only goes so far. To provide a satisfying definition that will stand up to criticism, a good writer follows up the negative with the positive.

Formal Definition—If definition is only part of your essay—a starting point for discussion and a point of reference—you can probably provide a formal definition without having argue about it much further.

Dictionary definitions are good examples of "formal" definition: They identify the words being defined. They provide background about word histories. They classify words as nouns, verbs, adjectives, or other classes of words. And they distinguish words from other, similar words. For your essay, the formal definition might be of a broader term, such as "Game Theory" or "focus-group testing" that you won't find in a dictionary, but you'd write the definition in much the same way:

Formal definition: What is the term being defined?
What are the term's origins?
How is it classified?
What makes it different from other similar terms?

Extended Definition—With an "extended definition," you're arguing about the definition itself, so you need to look at it from a number of different points of view and at greater length. An example of an extended definition might be a SAT essay assignment that asks you to discuss the concept of "home," and what it means to you. Here are some of the questions you could ask yourself in such an essay:

Extended definition: What is the formal definition?
What does the dictionary say?
What does your experience say?
What does society say?
What is the ideal?
What is the practical reality?
What are good examples?
What are comparisons and contrasts?
What are causes and effects?
What processes are involved?
What classifications can you make?

As you can see, some of the questions can be answered by components

IV: Writing the College Essay

like narration and description, comparison and contrast, classification, cause and effect, and process that we reviewed earlier in this chapter.

Stipulated Definition—Just as lawyers in a court case sometimes agree to save time by "stipulating" to a certain piece of evidence—agreeing that it's a fact without going to the trouble of proving it—you can sometimes stipulate a definition in an essay. For example, rather than delving into an extended definition that a term like "peace in Iraq" would require, you might be able to frame it as something that you can practically argue about. For example:

Threshold: Story of the controversial reception of Upton Sinclair's *The Jungle*. **FORMAL DEFINITION:** Muckrakers were a brief movement among early 20th Century journalists	**Agent**: Is the muckraking model still influential?	**Plan**: History of muckraking in magazines and newspapers.
Plan: Cause/effect discussion of how today's information age poses new challenges: modern "muckraking" journalism in blogs and its debt to the original muckrakers.	**Plan**: Reception of muckraking fiction vs. nonfiction among politicians, journalists, and intellectuals	**Plan**: Fiction of D.G. Phillips and Upton Sinclair
Takeaway: When today's writers and progressive politicians advocate for the interests of working americans, we should thank the first Muckrakers.		

Figure 21.8. Example of Plan for Essay on "Muckraking Journalism."

21. Plan

Let's stipulate, for the purposes of this argument, that "Peace in Iraq" means successfully establishing a permanent, stable government that doesn't require outside intervention to prop it up.

This kind of definition solves a lot of problems. But it also invites disagreement and only works well in certain limited situations. For instance, if your essay's focus is on ways to reduce American casualties in an Iraqi civil war, where a nuanced definition of "peace" isn't as important, the stipulated definition may work just fine. But, if your essay promises to examine the question of whether "true peace" is possible in Iraq, you'd simply be begging the question (see pg. 228) if you stipulated a definition.

The Definition Essay

A definition essay like that in Figure 21.8 typically employs the following structure:

- **Threshold/Agent**—Interests the reader and introduces terms (perhaps a formal definition), and makes a promise about what the essay will do, or states argumentative thesis.
- **Plan**—Expands on the basic definition and employs component plans such as comparison, cause, classification, or narrative to elaborate on the definition and argue for it.
- **Takeaway**—Sums up, predicts, recommends, or restates thesis.

22

Conclusion and Takeaway

Life is the art of drawing sufficient conclusions from insufficient premises. —Samuel Butler

The worst conclusions are those that come up with the wrong answer, but close behind are those that bore the reader by mechanically repeating or summarizing the thesis. If you've already stated your conclusions in your thesis, why would you want to put the very same language in your conclusion? At the least, you should find another way of saying it.

The traditional way to write conclusions is to restate your thesis. Note the word *restate*. It is not the same as *repeat*. Simply repeating your thesis insults the intelligence of your reader, and suggests that you're not really working very hard as a writer. *Restate*, in this context, means to convey the same basic idea *using different words*.

There's plenty to recommend this traditional approach. It drives home your main point and shows how your argument backs it up. It's a lot better than allowing the reader to finish your essay and wonder what your point was.

So go ahead, restate your thesis in your conclusion. It's a good way to get a "B." But if you aim higher, try thinking of your conclusion differently. Think of it as a *takeaway*.

By calling it a takeaway, you automatically think about your reader: *What will the reader take away from my essay?* That's a great start, because it forces you to think of your conclusion as an *action* rather than a place marker.

Remember what you learned back in Chapter 7 about emphasis—the two most emphatic places in an essay are the beginning and the end. The end of your essay should not be an afterthought, a mere restatement tacked onto the back for form's sake. It should make things happen.

So, what makes a conclusion memorable—what makes it something that you might take away with you and reflect on later, after having read it?

22. Conclusion and Takeaway

At the very least, your essay should end with a sense of *closure*—that you have thoroughly considered the topic and come to a reasonable conclusion about it. A takeaway is connected to that sense of closure: although it shouldn't introduce some wholly new claim that was never really considered in the essay, it can offer a fresh thought for the reader to take away about the topic that it has just covered. And it shouldn't just repeat the thesis.

Ways to End Your Essay

The following list of techniques and ideas for ending an essay isn't exhaustive—your imagination can certainly find other good ways to offer a takeaway.

1. **Thesis Conclusion**

   If your agent, or thesis, made a straightforward claim, you can conclude the paper by echoing that claim using new language. For example, suppose your agent or thesis claimed that

   > William Butler Yeats, though often viewed in the light of literary modernism, can best be understood as a part of the generation known as "Georgian Poets."

   Your conclusion might offer the following idea to take away:

   > As we have seen, Yeats reacted to the same things that Georgian Poets did—war, the loss of a more genteel way of life, nostalgia for religious and cultural certainties—but he gave those themes a distinctively modern and Irish twist that elevated his poems far above the often mediocre Georgian mainstream.

2. **Provocative Afterthought**

   One good way to end an essay, after you've made the case for your thesis, is by offering a concluding thought for the reader to take away from the experience. It should be closely related to the topic of your essay, but it might be something new, that you haven't specifically talked about. For instance, an essay that sought to prove that Donald Trump played fast and loose with the truth in his campaign rhetoric might offer its final claim, and then add the following afterthought:

   > President Richard Nixon is often remembered for his famous quote, "I am not a crook." President Bill Clinton is remembered for protesting, "I did not have sexual relations with that woman, Miss Lewinsky." It seems likely

IV: Writing the College Essay

that President Donald Trump will be remembered for some similar scandalous statement. We just don't know what it is yet.

3. **Compelling Quote or Reference to a Source**

    Sometimes you come across a quote from one of your sources that really distills the point you've been arguing in your essay. If you go this route, make sure that the quote is interesting in and of itself, and not just something that you could say better in a paraphrase. For instance, you might end an essay about political campaign rhetoric by arguing your thesis, that when we talk about political language, we often end up quoting the extremists, rather than the mainstream. Then you could bring in the following:

    > Or, as blogger Kevin Drum has observed, "[B]oth sides should try to respond to the standard issue folks on the other side, rather than pretending that they're all represented by the loudest, most extreme voices. It's easy to mount arguments against the extremists, but those arguments never actually persuade anyone."

4. **Question to Ponder**

    A "rhetorical question" is a question that provides its own answer—that the reader already knows the answer to. Sometimes it works well to end your essay with a rhetorical question, the answer to which should be obvious from the context of the paper. Asking a real question, one that you don't know the answer to, can work too, but is a little riskier, as your reader may resent you for not answering it in your paper. Here's an example, from an essay arguing that Amazon.com has already changed the way Americans shop:

    > In the 1950s and '60s, a staple image from American films was the local paperboy tossing the bundled news of the day onto the American doorstep. Will future movies, showing life in suburban America, show footage of Amazon drones delivering packages to the front porch?

5. **Answer to an Opening Question**

    As noted in Chapter 20, one of the strategies for writing an introduction is to ask a question that the essay will answer. If you've followed that strategy, your conclusion is easy: Answer the question! The trick to making this work, though, is to ask an opening question that requires more than a "yes" or "no" answer. An essay that ends, *So, the answer to the question with which this essay began, is "no,"* isn't a very strong conclusion. Rather, you want your answer to be in the form of a discursive

22. Conclusion and Takeaway

sentence—a thesis statement, perhaps, if you wrote a paper where the thesis appears at the end. Here's an example in which the opening of the paper asked the following question: *This paper will explore the question, "Why has pilgrimage been such an enduring metaphor for human life?"* The paper ends with the following:

> As we have seen, the elements of pilgrimage—struggle, a sense of penance, a search for something that matters—resonate with the journey that each of us takes from birth to death. In a sense, we are all pilgrims, and the metaphor of pilgrimage is one that helps us understand our lives.

6. Rebuttal

Just as you might open your essay by rebutting a controversial or wrong-headed view, you can end your essay that way too (though you probably want to avoid both beginning and ending with a rebuttal). Using the rebuttal strategy, you find something that someone else has said and illustrate how your essay has shown it to be wrong. Here's an example.

> Trump's apologists, like Fox News's Sean Hannity, argue that there is nothing wrong with the many contacts his administration has had with Russia. But, as this paper has demonstrated, in fact a pattern has emerged suggesting that Trump's longtime business connections with the corrupt Russian government are actually putting America's leading position in world affairs at risk.

7. Analogy or Parallel Case

As with introductions, finding a good analogy for the thing you've been arguing about can be a good way to end an essay. Here's an analogy used to wrap up an essay on the Obama administration's accomplishments:

> As I've shown, history will likely judge Obama to have been a consequential president. But just as the confusing end of the 2017 Academy Awards managed to obscure the artistic triumph of *Moonlight*, when *La-La-Land* was mistakenly announced as Best Picture, the many accomplishments of Obama's eight years in office are now being overlooked amidst the tumult and confusion of President Trump's dramatic election and chaotic first 100 days in office.

8. Confession or Personal Note

Your unsupported opinion is probably not appropriate for a college paper, but you can bring in personal experience to drive home an argument to which your own experience is relevant, as in the case of this essay on the importance of travel in broadening a person's horizons.

IV: Writing the College Essay

My own experience supports what the research shows, that travel gives a young person more perspective. I know I will never forget that first morning, waking up in the little English town of Rye, and walking through its strange, narrow, medieval streets. I knew at that moment how much about the world I didn't know—and how much I wanted to spend the rest of my life finding it out.

9. Link Back to the Opening Paragraph

If you began your essay with an image, or question, or quotation, or scenario, a good strategy is to circle back to it in your conclusion. Suppose, for instance, that you began an essay on writing style by quoting E. B. White's memorable statement, "Young writers often suppose that style is a garnish for the meat of prose, a sauce by which a dull dish is made palatable." Your essay might conclude as follows:

> E. B. White's much-quoted observation about style being more than a garnish on the "dull dish" of prose still seems to mark students' attitudes toward it. We equate employing fancy words and lofty sentences with good writing, when more often it is those who write the most plainly and clearly who will take home the prizes.

10. Answering the "Who Cares" and "So What" Questions

This technique is fairly obvious—moving from the concluding thesis to a statement about why it's important:

> So, as this paper has shown, by politicizing the Federal Reserve Board and making it too sensitive to the changing winds of presidential politics, we risk weakening and blinding the one institution capable of keeping America from suffering another economic debacle like those of 1928 and 2008.

11. Redefining a Key Term

An interesting twist to throw in at the end of an essay, particularly an argument of definition, is one of redefinition. The writer takes a key word from the definition and reinterprets it in a way that drives home the main point of the essay:

> This essay has examined the idea of wilderness in four American writers. But, in the end, for all four of them the true wilderness was within, as each struggled to come to terms with the part of himself that did not belong to civilized society. Each writer, in a sense, carried the wilderness with him whether hobnobbing with socialites in the city or risking death from exposure atop a lonely mountain in Maine or from wild animals encountered on safari in Africa.

12. Broader Implications of Your Thesis

22. Conclusion and Takeaway

Sometimes your thesis is fairly narrow, and makes a limited point, but one that suggests a broader, more generally applicable topic. This can take the form of a call for more research to be done on the broader topic, or merely nod to the broader topic, as in the following example:

> Cheryl Strayed's *Wild* thus tells the story of a writer dealing with the loss of her mother and the destructively wild, grief-stricken path it set her on. More than that, though, it is about a woman finding the strength within herself to move on, step after step, into a world where she can live life on her own terms.

No "B.S." About

Ending Your Paper

The conclusion, or takeaway, drives home your point. Since it's at the end of your paper, it's in the most emphatic position. It's what your readers will take away with them. Don't waste the opportunity.

1. **Restate your thesis, don't just repeat it.**
   Find a new way of saying what you said in your statement of agency, or thesis, early in the paper. The difference, of course, is that at the end of your paper your reader has seen all of your evidence and arguments, so you have, ideally, proven your point.
2. **Answer the "so what?" question.**
   Don't assume that your reader will understand the significance of what you've shown. Make sure that the takeaway points out the significance of what you've shown in your paper.
3. **Satisfy your reader.**
   If the introduction and agent of a paper promised something to readers, the conclusion should show how the evidence of the paper satisfies it. It should end with a sense of finality and completion.
4. **Don't introduce wholly new ideas.**
   While it's fine to bring in a final example or quotation that proves your point, resist the urge to end your paper with a wholly new idea that you haven't discussed in the body of the paper.
5. **In long essays, wrap up and make sense of what's been presented**
   In a long essay, your readers may forget your thesis and the way in

which your evidence and arguments support it. The conclusion offers you a chance to gently remind them of what the paper has shown. You don't need to do this is great detail, but it doesn't hurt to rehash some of the key points before you get to your takeaway point. This is especially true if your paper is on a highly technical subject.

23

A Short Chapter on Titles

I like titles that are a little difficult, because it's kind of counterintuitive. —Charlie Kaufman

Most college writers compose the title last, and often don't give it much thought. But your professor will insist you write a title for your papers, and not because he just feels like making your life miserable. Let's figure out why.

Look at the title to this chapter. It could have been "Titles," which would have been much simpler. Why dress it up?

For one thing, "Titles" would have been boring. Sure, it would have been to the point, but that's about it. By calling it "A Short Chapter on Titles," your author promises you several things: (1) that titles are worth their own chapter (if a short one); (2) that it may seem a little silly to devote an entire chapter to titles; and (3), that he has a sense of humor about it. The result? The chapter seems to promise to be short, useful, and maybe even a little funny.

So, maybe you're more likely to read the chapter.

As news headline writers will tell you, a good title vastly increases the chance that someone will actually read an article or an essay. Sure, in the case of a college essay, you can be pretty sure that your professor will read it whether there's a title or not, but studies have shown that a good title actually increases reader comprehension too. And you definitely want your professor to comprehend what you're writing about.

Your professors mostly want you to write papers in the format that academic journals require for publication, even if you're never going to try to get your paper published. They do it because really good papers sometimes do get published, and because they want you to learn the conventions of academic publishing, both to help your research and to help you take your own papers seriously, as a part of the larger academic conversation on the topic. Titles are a key part of that.

IV: Writing the College Essay

A good title does the following things:

- Announces the topic of your paper for a reader who might be skimming for information on that subject
- Suggests the findings and conclusions
- Addresses the "so what?" question

That's a lot to pack into a short line of type. Let's look at some examples of titles that do and don't work.

Eighteen Titles—Which Is Best?

Read the following list of eighteen titles, all turned in as argumentative research papers by a first-year writing class that focused on the theme of food. Which among them makes you want to read the paper? Which tells you what the paper's really about? Which needs more information? Which needs to be more concise and to the point?

1. *Organic v. Conventionally Grown Foods: Which Is Better for Your Health and Budget?*
2. *You Are What You Eat: Does Food Affect One's Mood?*
3. *The Diet and Its Effect on Childhood Behavior*
4. *Eat to Grow*
5. *Hungry for Acceptance: Societal and Biological View on Anorexia Nervosa*
6. *The Dancer's Struggle to be Perfect*
7. *Freshman Fifteen: Fact or Fiction?*
8. *Food: Is It as Safe as We Think?*
9. *We Are What We Eat, America.*
10. *A Look at the Correlation between Overeating and Mental Disorders through the Lens of Food Addiction and Obesity*
11. *Are Fad Diets Beneficial?*
12. *Title*
13. *Gluten-Free: Trend or Trick?*
14. *A Food-Conscious and Fashion-Conscious World*
15. *Is Childhood Obesity That BIG of an Issue; Should Fast Food Be Blamed?*
16. *Childhood Obesity: The Effects and What Can Be Done to Fix This Issue*

23. A Short Chapter on Titles

17. *The Effectiveness of a Nutrition Education Program in K–12 School Systems*
18. *Modernization and Innovation to Food Processing: Contamination Caused by New Technologies*

The worst of the titles is 12, where the writer never got around to composing a title at all. You can see the problem: you have no idea what the paper is about, and whether you'd want to read it.

Some of the titles are too vague. Titles 4, 9, and 14 try so hard to be intriguing that they leave the argument of the paper unclear. One might be about nutrition, one about American dietary habits, and one about fashionable foods, but that's just a guess, and the "So what?" question remains unanswered. Title 10 is quite wordy, but remains vague too—readers will wonder, "So what?"

Several titles in the group, 1, 2, 7, 8, 11, 13, and 15 employ the technique of asking a question, the answer to which will presumably be in the paper. It's a good way to make a title lively, but it gets overused, as you can see here. And, a research paper's title should at least suggest the answer: a reader scanning number 8, for example, is presented with a disturbing question: Is the food we eat safe? But, there's no suggestion of an answer. Safe from what? It seems somewhat sensationalistic—the kind of title you'd find in a tabloid newspaper rather than an academic paper.

Many of the tiles employ the common and useful academic trick of a colon (:) or semicolon (;) that adds a subtitle to their main title. It's a good idea. Unfortunately, in most of the cases above, the subtitle merely repeats the idea of the main title. Subtitles should *expand on* the main title, providing additional information. Title 5 does an excellent job of this, though it could be improved slightly by making the subtitle suggest the conclusions of the paper, rather than just the problem. Title 6 is specific and interesting, but needs a colon and a subtitle such as "Body Image Problems Vex Performers" to suggest the findings of the paper.

Title 18 has the right idea and gives a good sense of what the problem is (answering the "so what?" question), but it's wordy and dull. Still, for a research paper on food technologies, it's appropriate. It could be improved, perhaps, by adding some action: "Contamination Issues Bedevil Modern Food Processing Technology."

The best titles in the group, 3, 16, and 17, are fairly straightforward and give a clear sense of what the paper is about. They are serious and focused on the main point of the paper. Even those, however, could be improved by giving a clearer sense of the paper's argument.

IV: Writing the College Essay

NOTE: *These eighteen titles were all written for a formal argumentative research paper. If you're writing a paper that is more subjective and less focused on research, you may succeed with a title that is more informal in tone than the ones in this group. This is particularly true of creative projects and short papers where you're asked to react to an idea or subject. Remember, as noted in Chapter 3, the more scientific and scholarly the paper, the more formal the tone.*

Titles Shouldn't Be an Afterthought

So, titles are far more than decoration. They focus the reader's attention, help comprehension, provide what a reader looking for information needs to decide whether they're on his topic, and set the tone for the entire paper. In short, they deserve as much attention on the writer's part as the introduction, the thesis, or the takeaway of the essay. Make your titles lively, active, to the point, and suggestive of your findings. They deserve to be well written, not just tacked on before you turn the paper in.

No "B.S." About

Titles

Your title is the first thing your reader will see. If you're writing for a broad audience, the title may determine whether your essay gets read or gets skipped. If you're writing just for professors, the title will prepare them to judge what is to follow. In either case, it could be the most important bit of writing in the whole paper.

A good title does the following:

- Catches the reader's attention (If published, this means including keywords that will flag it in computer searches)
- Orients the reader to what the paper will address
- Identifies your attitude or approach to the subject

Tips on Writing Good Titles

1. The more scientific and scholarly the topic, the longer the title tends to be

23. A Short Chapter on Titles

Short, evocative, catchy titles work well for critical essays and arguments. Essays or papers that are scientific or scholarly lend themselves to longer, more discursive titles.

2. **If your paper has an attitude, your title should too**

   Not all papers are written with a straight, serious academic face. If you're writing something that's funny, satirical, angry, happy, or argumentative, that should be reflected in your title. A serious research paper deserves a serious title, but a subjective, opinionated essay's title should reflect the tone of the paper.

3. **A colon (subtitle) lets you have it both ways**

   Using a colon is a good way to link a catchy or fun main title with a serious or explanatory subtitle.

4. **Try picking an image or concrete detail out of the essay**

   Sometimes it works well to pick a dramatic or memorable quote or detail from the body of the paper that will serve to grab the reader's attention in the title. This technique works well when combined with a colon and a subtitle that explains it.

5. **Try beginning with a question**

   Although, as seen earlier in the chapter, this can be overused, try beginning with a question, such as journalism's Who? What? Where? When? Why? or How? Or try a question that begins with "Is" or "Does." Often questions work well when combined with a subtitle that explains what the essay will do.

6. **Try a title that begins with "on" or an "-ing" word**

   Titles such as "On Writing Titles" or "Writing a Good Title" can be effective if your strategy is to orient the reader to what the paper will address. They are particularly good for topics that seek to explain a subject.

24

Revision: The Second Look

> *Time for you and time for me,*
> *And time yet for a hundred indecisions,*
> *And for a hundred visions and revisions,*
> *Before the taking of a toast and tea.*
> —T. S. Eliot

This final chapter focuses on revision. It's not last because it's unimportant, but because it's typically the last thing that you do before turning in your paper. If grades are meaningful to you, remember that students who allow themselves time to revise their papers almost always make their papers better.

Revised drafts are certainly the place to proofread for spelling and grammar, but they're far more than that. They're your chance to take a second look at your ideas.

Give yourself time to revise. A great enemy of good writing is rushing to get it done at the last minute—that's when you'll trot out the clichés and careless sentences.

In general, it's a three-step process: (1) start with big questions; then (2) improve your transitions; and finally (3) dive into the details.

Review the Big Picture

As Chapter 1 noted, good writers review their paper in three ways: *Ruminating*—reviewing what they intended to say and making sure they've made their key points; *Empathizing*—rereading what they've just written from the point of view of their audience to see if it makes sense; and *Comparing*—deciding whether what they meant to say is what the reader is actually hearing.

Ruminating—The word literally means chewing over the ideas again to

24. Revision: The Second Look

get more out of them, as a cow chews its cud over and over again in the process of digestion. Look at the big picture first. Reread what you've written with a skeptical eye and ask yourself the following questions:

- Does my introduction bring readers to the argument's threshold, where they will be engaged by the main issue of the paper?
- How could I do a better job of engaging the reader's interest and imagination? (See Chapter 19)
- Is my plan clear—does it walk readers through the argument and ideas in an orderly way? (See Chapter 21)
- Have I supported major claims with data and good reasons?
- Do I need to get better data to support my claims?
- Do my warrants make sense? (See Chapter 10)

Empathizing—Put yourself in your reader's shoes for a moment. That reader doesn't know what's in your head (your house of ideas). This is a good time to actually get your friends to read your paper and talk to you about its ideas; they shouldn't just be proofreading, though! Quiz your readers to see if they really understand your argument. Try to get them to restate your argument in their own words. Look for where they get it mixed up and which ideas need clarifying. That should tell you something. Then ask yourself these questions:

- Have I anticipated the skepticism of readers who don't agree with my argument? If not, try to anticipate skeptical questions.
- Does my paper sufficiently refute objections to my point (See refutations, Chapter 12) to win over the skeptical reader?
- Can I concede certain good points of the other side without undercutting my argument?
- What terminology will be unclear to the reader?
- Have I fallen into the trap of abstraction (Chapter 5) instead of being specific about my ideas and research?
- What background information does the reader need?
- Have I found convincing authorities and data to support my argument?
- Do I rely on my own unsubstantiated claims and opinions? (Chapter 9)
- Do the points make logical sense?
- Do I need more research or analysis to support my thesis? (Chapter 10)

Comparing—Reread your paper with an eye to comparing what you want to say with what a reader is likely to take away from it. Pay particular attention to your thesis, or agent, and your takeaway. Ask yourself these questions:

- Did my paper make a promise to the reader about what it's discussing? If so, did it fulfill that promise and provide my argumentative answers to the questions it raised?
- Have I cherry-picked only the data that supports my argument? If so, how can I account for facts and arguments that don't fit my thesis?
- Is most of my paper about the points raised in my thesis and takeaway, or does it get off track?
- Have I spent too much time presenting data without sufficiently analyzing it or arguing about it?
- Have I fallen into the Objective Style (Chapter 2) in an effort to B.S. my reader that I'm authoritative? If so, does my argument seem thin when written plainly?

Re-Examine Your Transitions

After you've asked these big-picture questions, spend a few minutes improving the flow of your paper—look at its transitions in particular. Remember that you want to avoid having your paper seem like a list: it should move smoothly and logically from one topic to the next. Here are some ways to do it gracefully:

Restate or echo earlier points—Look at the paragraph above. Notice how it begins by referring to what came before, and then shifts to its main subject? That's often a good transition technique. Pick something from the previous paragraph and build on it.

Use transitional and connecting words—Here's where you can add words and phrases that indicate that you're building and expanding on what has come before:

Similarly	On the other hand	Thus
By extension	Conversely	Such
Just as	In this way	Hence
Secondly	Consequently	However

Argue with yourself—If your paragraph has made an assertion, the next paragraph may want to argue with it or expand on it. For example, this paragraph could have begun as follows: "Although transitional words can work well, sometimes you want something more dramatic."

Refer back to your plan—If you're using a plan such as comparison, classification, process analysis, or cause and effect (Chapter 22), think of yourself

24. Revision: The Second Look

as the real estate agent leading clients through the house of ideas who is constantly reminding them of the layout. Consider using phrases such as, "By way of comparison," or "A second class of transitional phrase is …," or "The next step in the process is …," and the like.

Improve Your Sentences and Words

Finally, once you've looked at the big picture and examined your transitions, it's time to bring in Richard Lanham's "Paramedic Method" (Chapter 2) and start improving your sentences. Root out the Objective Style wherever it has taken hold. Look for repetitious phrases that don't add anything new. Think about the action of the sentence or paragraph—what's it trying to *do*? Does it succeed?

Review Part I of this book. Revision is where you can really put those lessons about word choice, tone, and rhythm into effect. Now's the time to find the perfect word, or the witty phrase, or the enlightening figure of speech. Revision on the word and sentence level should be where you show your true skill as a writer. Look for the dead or merely serviceable phrase and try replacing it with something with energy and verve. Have fun. If you do this assiduously, pretty soon your paper will sound like *you*—it will be written in your distinctive style.

Before You Turn Your Paper In

Having drafted and revised your paper, you'll probably be eager to send it to your professor. It's tempting, at this point, to view your paper as a thing—an artifact that you've produced using your tools and skills as a writer. It's done with, and you can now put all that work behind you and move on to the next assignment. That's perhaps inevitable, but it's a mistake.

Now's the time to step back from your paper and think about it in terms of the larger process—as something that's part of your entire college experience. How does it fit in? What have you learned by writing it? What more do you want to know? How can you apply what you've learned to your larger goals for being in college?

Remember that the process of writing college papers isn't just a pointless exercise that your professors inflict on you. As skeptical as you may be about

IV: Writing the College Essay

it (and skepticism is a good way to approach your college experience in general), it's meant to do something more than get you to regurgitate class lectures. The point of putting you through the paper-writing process is making you think beyond the mere realm of facts and data, important as they are, and start making connections.

Writing college papers doesn't happen in a vacuum. It's part of discovering who you can be. If you approach the discipline that way, and look at the college experience not as an ordeal but rather as an opportunity, you'll be on the right track. Pretty soon you'll find that all of the subjects and skills you've learned during your college years have become part of you—changing you, pointing you toward the future.

No footnotes will be required. And no B.S.

Appendix I

Logical Fallacies

Logical fallacies, as described in Chapter 13, are flawed arguments that appeal to means of persuasion other than valid logic to persuade the listener. Some are very compelling. None are, strictly speaking, logical. A good writer learns to avoid them. Here are some of the best-known and most common fallacies:

Fallacy of Character (*Ad Hominem*)—A claim based on attacking the "man" (Latin: *homo*) rather than the merits of the argument. It assumes that because a person has a bad character or a bias, any argument made by that person is wrong, regardless of its logic.

> Michael argues that abortion is morally wrong, but you can't trust anything he says on the subject because he's a Catholic priest, which means he's just a mouthpiece for the Pope.
>
> President Clinton lied about having sex with an intern, so you shouldn't believe anything he says.

***Tu Quoque* Fallacy**—Literally, "You, too"; like the character fallacy, this claim ignores the merits of an argument and focuses on the limitations of the person making it. Since the arguer is flawed, it reasons, the argument must be too.

> "Why should I listen to you telling me to quit smoking? You're a pack-a-day smoker yourself."
>
> "He can't sue me for copyright infringement! His book is completely plagiarized."

Fallacy of Authority (*Ad Vericundiam*)—Literally, an appeal "to authority": a claim that assumes an authoritative person can't be wrong, even when the situation differs, or when that person isn't speaking in his area of expertise.

> Scientists who deny God's existence should listen to Albert Einstein, who explained the purposefulness of Creation by saying, "God doesn't throw dice" with the universe.

Appendix I

> President Bush was justified in denying habeas corpus rights to enemy combatants at Guantanamo; after all, Abraham Lincoln suspended habeas corpus during the Civil War, so there's a good precedent.

Fallacy of Fear (*Ad Baculum*)—Literally an appeal "to the stick"; a claim in which intimidation rather than logic provides compelling persuasion.

> If in your lectures you insist on arguing that Evolution is proven science, rather than just a theory, we will organize a public protest and boycott your classes.
>
> Any student who engages in hate speech should be expelled from the university.

Fallacy of the Unknown (*Ad Ignorantiam*)—Literally, an appeal "to ignorance." A claim contending that something is correct because it's based on information not known (and thus irrefutable).

> Despite all the recent reports of people seeing the supposedly extinct Ivory-billed woodpecker, no one has yet verified a sighting. Therefore the bird must really be extinct.
>
> The reason I know that there's a God is that no one has ever proven He doesn't exist.

Fallacy of Pity (*Ad Misericordiam*)—Literally, an appeal "to pity"; a claim based on empathy rather than logic.

> We should all do what we can to stop global warming, or else the polar bear will become extinct.
>
> President Bush was right to commute Lewis Libby's jail sentence; the poor man has suffered enough for his country.

Fallacy of Popularity (*Ad Populum*)—Literally, an appeal "to the crowd"; a claim contending that the majority is always right.

> Americans overwhelmingly think that our decision to invade Iraq was immoral, so clearly we were wrong to do so.
>
> How can you oppose the death penalty when most Americans support it?

Begging the Question Fallacy—Circular reasoning. A claim "begs the question" when it bases its justification on the very thing being argued about.

> Obviously, polygamy should be illegal. It's against the law in all Western nations.
>
> Alcohol and tobacco products should be regulated like other drugs.

The Loaded Question Fallacy—Like begging the question, it assumes an argument that hasn't been proven under the cover of a question about something else. Also known as the "complex question fallacy," or "fallacy of many questions."

> Are you still wasting your money on pornography?
>
> Students at this university have sophisticated tastes. How else can you explain the success of the Starbucks at the library, or the Perrier in the vending machines?

Non Sequitur Fallacies—Literally, "does not follow"; a false claim is based on true claims that don't prove it. There are several varieties, including "Denying the Antecedent" and "Affirming the Consequent."

> We can solve the unemployment problem if we do a better job of educating students.
>
> Of course James Joyce tells good stories—he's Irish, isn't he?
>
> We will stop the killing if we ban all handguns.
>
> You shouldn't do work that you don't love.

Distribution Fallacies—These mistaken inferences include *division fallacies* and *composition fallacies*. A division fallacy claims that because a group has certain properties (for example, the average family has 1.8 children), every member of that group has those properties (therefore Family X must have 1.8 children). A composition fallacy claims that because each member of a group has a certain property (each player is the best at his position), therefore the group has a similar property (therefore Team X must be the best team).

> Men have beards and hairy backs, so therefore Adam will have a beard and a hairy back.
>
> I built my bicycle out of the highest-priced components, so it's the most expensive bicycle that money can buy.
>
> We ordered the pizza with cheese, anchovies, and pepperoni, so any slice will therefore have cheese, anchovies, and pepperoni on it.
>
> Students at this University typically have high SAT scores and a high GPA, so obviously Ellen must have had great scores and a high GPA or she wouldn't be going here.

Equivocation Fallacy—A fallacy of ambiguity. The same word means two different things, but the claim asserts only one meaning.

> Abbott: Who's on first, What's on second, I Don't Know is on third...
> Costello: That's what I want to find out.
>
> You live in a commune, right? So you must be a communist.

Appendix I

Hasty Generalization Fallacies—These include several kinds of fallacies, including the biased statistics fallacy, insufficient statistics fallacy, and narrow sampling fallacy. Claims depends on statistics that have not been controlled for sampling bias, or are too narrow a sample.

> An Internet-like poll revealed today that Americans overwhelmingly prefer to submit their income taxes electronically.
>
> We set out traps baited with stinky cheese; based on that, we conclude that the only animals roaming our neighborhood at night are mice, dogs, and raccoons.
>
> I dislike all Americans. Of the ten I've met here in Baghdad, nine have been ready to shoot me.
>
> Is there a food hygiene crisis in North Carolina fast-food restaurants? Three of five visited by Eyewitness News had Grade B sanitation ratings, or lower.

False Analogy—Although argument by analogy can be an effective technique, the analogy must be carefully chosen. The claim of a false analogy is that A=B, so therefore the lessons of A also apply to B. No analogy is perfect, but if it's clear that the analogy is a bad match, it loses its rhetorical effect.

> The lesson of Viet Nam is clear for those debating Iraq policy: If we leave, it will be overrun by Al Qaeda.
>
> Children are like nails: You have to whack 'em sometimes if you want them to stay put.

Guilt by Association—Like the hasty generalization and red herring fallacies, guilt by association makes a claim based on an insufficiently supported sample, and attempts to divert attention from a more complicated question.

> George Bush and Dick Cheney got us into Iraq, and they're Republicans. You're Republican, so you must have supported them.
>
> The American Communist Party supported the Civil Rights movement. Martin Luther King was probably a communist too.

Irrelevant Conclusion Fallacy—Like the *non sequitur* and red herring fallacies, an irrelevant conclusion makes a claim that's not relevant to the evidence presented.

> "I support animal tests of new drugs because I don't want our children to suffer."
>
> Still, Dr. Hansen said, the former vice president's work may hold "imperfections" and "technical flaws." He pointed to hurricanes, an icon for Mr. Gore, who highlights the devastation of Hurricane Katrina and cites research suggest-

ing that global warming will cause both storm frequency and deadliness to rise. Yet this past Atlantic season produced fewer hurricanes than forecasters predicted (five versus nine), and none that hit the United States.[1]

Post Hoc Fallacy—From the Latin *post hoc ergo propter hoc* ("after this, therefore because of this"). This fallacy makes a claim about causation: since Y happened after X, X caused Y. But sometimes other factors were responsible, or certain conditions had to be in place for the event to take place.

Hurricane Katrina caused New Orleans to flood.
"The 9/11 attacks wouldn't have happened if President Bush had spent more time working to solve the conflict between the Israelis and Palestinians."

Slippery Slope Fallacy—A claim of causation, like the *post hoc* fallacy, that depends on the false analogy of a slippery slope. In fact, sometimes things aren't going downhill at all.

"Legalizing gambling is just the thin edge of the wedge. Once that's in place, organized crime will take over."
"Stop the subway fare increase, or pretty soon they'll be charging $10 just to ride across town."

Red Herring Fallacy—This fallacy makes a claim intended to divert attention from the merits of another claim, and gets its name from the practice of diverting hunting foxhounds by dragging rotten fish across the field ahead of them.

"Sure, having national health care is a popular idea. But the Democrats are making so many proposals that the whole thing is getting out of hand."
"The U.S. shouldn't sign the Kyoto protocols. The scientists who support doing so are all left wingers."

Straw Man Fallacy—Like the red herring fallacy, this claim aims to divert attention to another subject. Rather than attack a subject on its merits, the arguer constructs a "straw man" that can easily be knocked down.

"You say that the streets aren't a safe place for kids to play, but I say it's not good for them to keep them locked up inside all day."
"I don't think there's a God. If you want to know why I'm an atheist, just look at all the horrible things that have been done in the name of religion over the years."

---

1. William J. Broad, "From a Rapt Audience, a Call to Cool the Hype," *New York Times* (March 13, 2007).

Appendix I

The Two Wrongs Fallacy—A kind of "red herring"; rather than consider the merits of an ethical claim, the fallacy tries to justify wrong actions by claiming that the other party would have acted wrongly, given the chance.

> "I didn't return the money when they undercharged me because you can bet they wouldn't have refunded money to me if they'd overcharged me."
>
> "Capital punishment is only fair, since the person being executed is a killer."

The Gambler's Fallacy—The belief or claim that something random can be affected by other events, or that randomness itself is an assurance of a given outcome.

> "When I fly on an airplane, I always bring a bomb with me. The chances of an airplane having a bomb on it are very small, and certainly the chances of having two are almost none!"
>
> "The last two times you've flipped a coin, it came up 'tails.' I've got a feeling that it's going to be three in a row."

Appendix II

Style Guides

Now, I personally enjoy a really good footnote.—Ann Leckie

"Style" means two different things in the context of academic writing. We've covered the first in Part I of this book: *the way you write and express yourself.* But there's another meaning that gets nearly as much attention in academic papers: *the guidelines that you use for formatting and documenting your work.* The first refers to how you write, and the second refers to how you present your writing.

Newspaper reporters learn to write according to a set of conventions established by the Associated Press. *The Associated Press Stylebook* tells them, for instance, to use the word "allege" when referring to what police say about somebody they've caught red-handed: "Police allege that the man had the stolen watch when he was apprehended." The stylebook tells them to spell "A-list" with a hyphen. And, you also won't find anything about footnotes in the stylebook—they aren't used in news stories.

If you're going to be a journalist, or are going to be writing for newspapers or the Web, you need to learn the conventions of Associated Press style. It's an example of a "style guide" that is used in the larger world beyond the gates of your college.

Other examples of a real-world style guides can be found at most large companies, which have internal guidelines that employees have to follow when writing about the company and its products. A company like Coca-Cola, for instance, might instruct its writers to always include the "trademark registered" symbol when referring to Coke®.

In college, however, academicians use various style guides that are specific to their disciplines. If you are writing a paper in one of those disciplines, the professors expect you to use the appropriate style guide. Most college writing handbooks include sections that teach the basic ins and outs of academic styles. The following are four commonly encountered by students:

Appendix II

- **MLA Style**—Guidelines established by the Modern Language Association (MLA) for students writing papers in English and other areas of the humanities.
- **APA Style**—Guidelines established by the American Psychological Association (APA) for students writing papers in psychology and the social sciences.
- **CSE Style**—Guidelines established by the Council of Science Editors (CSE) for students writing papers in the biological sciences and other "hard sciences."
- **Chicago Style** (sometimes called "Turabian Style")—Guidelines established by the University of Chicago and widely used by academic presses for manuscripts and theses that will be published as books.

There are dozens more, but most undergraduate students only need to learn MLA and APA styles for papers in the humanities and sciences, respectively. Graduate students, particularly those publishing academic papers or writing in the sciences, may also need to learn CSE or Chicago style.

Why can't there just be one academic style? It's a reasonable question. The real answer is that different disciplines have traditions that they cling to stubbornly, and professors in those areas feel the traditions are too important to be determined by the convenience of the students who have to learn the various styles. From the student's point of view, it's a bogus reason. But, in fact, there are some good reasons, too.

MLA Style, for instance, is used by writers in the humanities, where the date of publication is not always the most crucial thing to know. An English article written about the poet John Donne in, say, 1921, can still have important critical ideas that scholars are referring to nearly a century later. The fact that it's an old article doesn't take away from the importance of what was said. So, MLA Style doesn't stress the date of publication. It's more concerned about the page number that a quote was taken from, and getting the capitalization and punctuation right.

On the other hand, in the sciences and social sciences, which see breakthrough ideas every year, the date of publication is very important. A geology article published in 1921 is likely to include ideas about the creation of continents that have been superseded by more recent discoveries and theories. APA and CSE styles, consequently, put a great deal of stress on when things were published, and they abbreviate authors names and change punctuation for conciseness.

Style Guides

Certain professors get very picky about this stuff; others will let you get by with something approximating the right form.[1] In any case, it's certainly worth learning the most common documentation style required by courses in your major subject (MLA style for English majors, for example).

A short book like this one doesn't have room to cover the differences in various academic styles in detail. Instead, this appendix will briefly outline some key features of four major style guides. Enjoy!

Modern Language Association (MLA) Style

One of the two most common documentation styles. MLA style uses parenthetical references in the text, instead of footnotes, and is picky about the punctuation and capitalization of sources. Unlike other styles, it pays a great deal of attention to the page or paragraph from which you're quoting material.

- In-text parenthetical references to quotations, paraphrases, or summaries include the author's name and the page number (or paragraph number) of the material being cited.
- Parenthetical references are often placed at the end of sentences or clauses, unless it is confusing to do so.
- If you mention the author's name in your text, do not include it in the parenthetical citation.
- Quotations more than four lines long should be indented as blocks, with no quotation marks.
- Punctuation marks come *after* the in-text parenthetical reference (except in the case of block quotes).
- Every in-text citation in your paper must refer to a corresponding entry in your list of works cited.
- Either footnotes or endnotes can be used, but only for explanatory information, not for bibliographic information.
- If you refer to the same source multiple times in a single paragraph, it is acceptable to use the "documentation sandwich" described in Chapter 16.
- Instead of "bibliography" or "references" at the end of the paper or article, MLA style includes an alphabetized list of "Works Cited." Each item in

---

1. If your professor is picky, beware of the automated citation generators that many library databases provide for online articles: they're notoriously inexact, and will fill your citations up with unnecessary URLs, improper abbreviations, and the like. Use them advisedly. It's safer to learn the rules and do it yourself.

Appendix II

the list should contain the following elements, unless they're unavailable from the source: author, title of source, title of container, other contributors, version, number, publisher, publication date, and location.
- *Sample in-text and bibliographic citations:*

  In-Text Citations—Use parentheses to identify up to three authors; use the first author's name and "et al." if there are four or more. If your sentence includes the author's name, don't put it in the parenthetical reference. Don't use commas or the abbreviation p. for page numbers. If you use an indirect quotation (someone quoted by your source), indicate it with ("qtd. in").

  > McDonald, Wearing, and Ponting studied thirty-nine participants who reported having a "peak experience" in the wilderness (370).

  > "[I]t was not until the 18th and 19th centuries that Western artists began to popularize the spiritual, restorative, health-giving benefits of natural settings" (McDonald, Wearing, and Ponting 372).

  > One participant in the study said, "I have revisited this place and still found myself in awe of the surroundings" (qtd. in McDonald, Wearing, and Ponting 381).

  Bibliographic Entries—Any source retrieved from the Web or electronic books or databases should be identified as "Web," and the date of access included. Print sources should be identified as "Print." URLs for Web sites are not required. Indicate the database that articles come from.

  Works Cited

  Hall, Dave, and Jon Ulrich. *Winter in the Wilderness: A Field Guide to Primitive Survival Skills.* Ithaca, NY: Cornell U P, 2015. *Ebrary.* Web. 12 Apr. 2017

  McDonald, Matthew G., Stephen Wearing, and Jess Ponting. "The Nature of Peak Experience In Wilderness." *Humanistic Psychologist* 37.4 (2009): 370–385. *Academic Search Premier.* Web. 12 Apr 2017.

  "Pacific Crest Trail: A Wild and Scenic Pathway from Mexico to Canada." Pacific Crest Trail Association. Web. 12 Apr. 2017.

  Strayed, Cheryl. *Wild: From Lost to Found on the Pacific Crest Trail.* New York: Vintage, 2012. Print.

American Psychological Association (APA) Style

The other major documentation style, APA style is commonly used in the sciences and social sciences. It uses parenthetical citations in the text, instead of footnotes, and pays a great deal of attention to the dates of sources.

Style Guides

- For in-text references, APA Style uses the author's last name and the year of publication, punctuated with a comma (Williams, 2017).
- Include the page number and an abbreviation for *page* or *pages* if you're quoting directly (Williams, 2017, p. 14).
- When sources have no page numbers, use a paragraph number (Smith, 2017, par. 25).
- In-text references appear directly after the relevant word or phrase, rather than at the end of a sentence or paragraph, and precede punctuation marks. If your text mentions the author's name, only the year of publication is required in the citation.
- Cite Web pages in text with author and date, if known. Use the title and the date as the in-text citation for anonymous sources. Shorten long titles.
- In-text citations should correspond to your reference list.
- Use n.d. (for "no date") in place of the year if sources aren't dated.
- If a parenthetic reference includes multiple authors' names, set the last one off with the & (ampersand) symbol. Use "and" if referring to multiple authors in the text.
- Long quotations (forty words or more) should be set off as block quotations, with no quotation marks.
- Instead of "works cited" or "bibliography" at the end of the paper or article, APA style includes an alphabetized list of "References."
- *Sample in-text and bibliographic citations:*

    In-Text Citations—In works with one or two authors, use parentheses to identify all of the authors; in works with three to five authors, identify all of them the first time you cite the source; subsequently, use the first author's name and "et al." If there are six or more authors, use the first author's name and "et al." If your sentence includes the author's name, don't put it in the parenthetical reference. Indirect sources (where you haven't read the original) should be identified by "as cited in."

    > Kover and Neuhauser (1988) suggest that given all the changes the health care industry will face, adapting the organization will be the greatest challenge administrators face.

    > "The education and training of health care professionals shape their identities, values, and norms of practice in certain ways that may either enhance or inhibit effective communication and collaboration…" (Clark, 1997, p. 442).

    > Maslow argues that the social needs "wax and wane on the strength of our personal relationships and our participation with others in the organization" (as cited in Bensen and Dundis 2003, p. 317).

Appendix II

Bibliographic Entries—Each item in the list of references should contain the following elements, unless they're unavailable from the source: Author (last name, initials only for first and middle names), Date of publication, title of article (capitalize only the first word of title and subtitle, and proper nouns), title of publication in italics, place of publication (for books), volume number in italics and issue number, page numbers of article, URL or DOI for online articles.

References

Benson, S.G., & Dundis, S.P. (2003) Understanding and motivating health care employees: integrating Maslow's hierarchy of needs, training and technology. *Journal of Nursing Management* 11, 315–320. doi: 10.1046/j.1365-2834.2003.00409.x

Clark P.G. (1997) Values in health care professional socialization: implications for geriatric education in interdisciplinary teamwork. *Gerontologist* 37 (4), 441–451.

Kover A.R. & Neuhauser D. (1988) *New Management in Human Services.* National Association of Social Workers, Silver Springs, MD.

Council of Science Editors (CSE) Style

CSE Style is a concise documentation style that abbreviates many entries. It offers three variations, depending on the conventions of the scientific discipline you're writing in (ask your professor); use the Citation Sequence System, the Citation Name System, or the Name-Year System for in-text references.

- In-text references stress the date of publication.
- In-text references appear directly after the relevant word or phrase, rather than at the end of a sentence or paragraph, and precede punctuation marks. If your text mentions the author's name, only the year of publication is required in the citation.
- For more than two authors, list the first author and "et al." Use just the title if there's no author.
- If there's no date, use the date you accessed it for online sources, and [date unknown] for print sources.
- *Sample in-text and bibliographic citations:*

Citation Sequence System. This system uses footnotes, then lists references at the end in the order that they're mentioned in the text:

These and the more exploratory box plots and graphs that give locally weighted regression lines[14] were performed in SYSTAT.[15]

Style Guides

[14]Cleveland WS, Devlin SJ. 1988. Locally weighted regression: an approach to regression analysis by local fitting. J Amer Stat Assoc 1988;83:597–610.
[15]Wilkinson L et al. SYSTAT for the macintosh, version 5.2. 1992 Evanston (IL) SYSTAT; 1992. 508 p.

Citation Name System. This system uses footnotes, then lists references in alphabetical order and numbers them:

These and the more exploratory box plots and graphs that give locally weighted regression lines[9] were performed in SYSTAT.[81]

---

[9]Cleveland WS, Devlin SJ. 1988. Locally weighted regression: an approach to regression analysis by local fitting. J Amer Stat Assoc 1988;83:597–610.

[Seventy-two other references are listed alphabetically.]

[81]Wilkinson L et al. SYSTAT for the macintosh, version 5.2. 1992 Evanston (IL) SYSTAT; 1992. 508 p.

Name-Year System. This system uses parentheses to list the name of the source in the text, then alphabetizes them at the end of the article under the heading "References":

These and the more exploratory box plots and graphs that give locally weighted regression lines (Cleveland and Devlin 1988) were performed in SYSTAT (Wilkinson et al. 1992).

References

Cleveland WS, Devlin SJ. 1988. Locally weighted regression: an approach to regression analysis by local fitting. J Amer Stat Assoc 1988;83:597–610.

[Seventy-two other references are listed alphabetically.]

Wilkinson L et al. SYSTAT for the macintosh, version 5.2. 1992 Evanston (IL) SYSTAT; 1992. 508 p.

Other Notes About CSE Style: The bibliographic citation doesn't include any periods or blank spaces for abbreviations of names. It only capitalizes the first word of the title, and doesn't use quotation marks. Journal names are abbreviated, and not italicized. Spaces following the date for journals are condensed.

University of Chicago (Chicago) Style (also called Turabian Style)

The University of Chicago Press's exacting and encyclopedic *Chicago Manual of Style* has become the standard for most academic presses, and

Appendix II

many commercial ones as well. Chicago's *A Manual for Writers of Research Papers, Theses, and Dissertations*, by Kate L. Turabian, boils the style guide down for academic writers. Consequently, dissertations and theses intended for publication are often formatted in Chicago Style. Some academic departments, particularly history departments, also require it for undergraduate papers.

Chicago style offers the choice of two systems. The notes and bibliography system, favored in humanities fields, features footnotes (or endnotes) and a bibliography at the end. The author-date system, favored in the sciences, briefly cites sources in the text, using parenthetical references, and a full list of references at the end.

Notes and Bibliography System. This system uses footnotes/endnotes in the text, then alphabetizes them at the end of the article under the heading "Bibliography."

- Fully document the first note for a source, giving all the publication information and the page number. On second reference, give only the author's last name, an abbreviated title, and the page number.
- When there are two or three authors, list all the names in the note and bibliography. For four or more authors, list all of the authors in the bibliography; in the note, list only the first author, followed by et al. ("and others").
- When you have two consecutive notes from the same source, use the Latin abbreviation *Ibid.* If it's the same source, but a different page number, add the page number.
- Notes and bibliographies are single-spaced. Indent the first line of notes. Bibliography entries have hanging indents of 0.5" Double-space between notes and bibliography entries.
- In the text, the note's number should be raised or superscripted; in the note itself, it is not raised or superscripted. A period and one space follow the number in notes.
- If you refer to the same source multiple times in a single paragraph, it is acceptable to use the "documentation sandwich" described in Chapter 16, using notes rather than parenthetical references.
- *Sample in-text and bibliographic citations:*

    At Heritage Village,[3] pilgrims to PTL entered what one scholar has called the "liminal state"[4]; Utterback describes that state by saying it is one in which "the pilgrims have left their familiar surroundings and have entered into unknown circumstances."[5]

Style Guides

3. Thomas C. O'Guinn and Russell W. Belk, "Heaven on Earth: Consumption at Heritage Village, USA," *Journal of Consumer Research* 16, no. 2 (1989): 228. https://doi.org/10.1086/209211
4. Kristine T. Utterback, "Saints and Sinners on the Same Journey; Pilgrimage as Ritual Process," *Medieval Perspectives* 15 (2000): 120.
5. Ibid. 123.

Bibliography

O'Guinn, Thomas C., and Russell W. Belk. "Heaven on Earth: Consumption at Heritage Village, USA." Journal of Consumer Research 16, no. 2 (1989): 227–238. https://doi.org/10.1086/209211

Utterback, Kristine T. "Saints and Sinners on the Same Journey; Pilgrimage as Ritual Process." *Medieval Perspectives* 15 (2000): 120–129.

Author-Date System. This system uses parenthetical references in the text, then alphabetizes them at the end of the article under the heading "Bibliography."

- Include the author's name(s) and date, along with the page number, in parenthetical references.
- If there are two or three authors, list the last names of all in the parenthetical reference. For four or more authors, list all of the authors in the reference list; in the text, list only the first author, followed by et al. ("and others")
- Bibliographies are alphabetized and single-spaced, with a hanging indent of 0.5" on the first line. Double-space between entries.
- The date should follow the author's name in bibliography entries.
- If you refer to the same source multiple times in a single paragraph, it is acceptable to use the "documentation sandwich" described in Chapter 16, using parenthetical references.
- *Sample in-text and bibliographic citations:*

    At Heritage Village (O'Guinn and Belk 1989, 228), pilgrims to PTL entered what one scholar has called the "liminal state" (Utterback 2000, 120); Utterback describes that state by saying it is one in which "the pilgrims have left their familiar surroundings and have entered into unknown circumstances" (123).

Bibliography

O'Guinn, Thomas C., and Russell W. Belk. 1989. "Heaven on Earth: Consumption at Heritage Village, USA." *Journal of Consumer Research* 16, no. 2: 227–238. https://doi.org/10.1086/209211

Utterback, Kristine T. 2000. "Saints and Sinners on the Same Journey; Pilgrimage as Ritual Process." *Medieval Perspectives* 15: 120–129.

Appendix III

Writing in the Sciences

> *Science is often hard to read. Most people assume that its difficulties are born out of necessity, out of the extreme complexity of scientific concepts, data and analysis. We argue here that complexity of thought need not lead to impenetrability of expression....* —George Gopen and Judith Swann, *American Scientist*

So, you're a science major, and you're probably saying to yourself, "None of this applies to me. I'm a scientist, and no one cares about writing in the sciences."

Bzzzt! Wrong. There's a lot of bad writing in the sciences, but scientists aren't happy about it. Just because you're not going to be an English major doesn't mean that you can blow off all the advice about good writing in this book. In fact, as we discussed in Chapter 2, since college is all about science, the burden of making complicated concepts clear and understandable weighs especially heavy on you.

That said, science offers some particular challenges to writers who want to communicate clearly, and its conventions sometimes seem to discourage good writing. It doesn't have to be that way. This appendix will explore some of those challenges, and suggest ways that you can be both a scientist and a good writer.

The Objective Style in Science

Part of the problem is that science teachers encourage scientific objectivity, and students get that mixed up with the Objective Style, which Chapter 2 of this book describes at length. If my work sounds scientific, the student reasons, it must *be* scientific.

Sorry, but that's B.S.

While scientific writing does discourage some of the subjectivity common to humanities disciplines, it still places a lot of emphasis on arguing and figuring out *who did what* and *what happened*. When you think of it, even a basic lab report answers just such a question—what happened? The fundamental need to understand those things doesn't change just because you're studying biology instead of history.

Anne E. Greene, author of *Writing Science in Plain English*, points out that studies have shown that scientists look for the same basic things that other readers do:

> [R]eaders look for a story about characters and actions; for strong verbs close to their subjects; for old information at the beginnings of sentences and new information at the ends; and for specific kinds of information in predictable places in paragraphs and documents.

Duke University's graduate school offers the following paragraph as an example of bad scientific writing:

> To understand human evolution, genomes from related primates are necessary. For example, identification of features common among primates or unique to humans will require several primate genomes. Fortunately, scientists can now do such genome-wide exploration; in the past 5 years, the community has released several nonhuman primate genome sequences.[1]

It certainly sounds very scientific. So, what's wrong with it? First of all, although it's about an action—comparing genomes—that's not stated clearly. Instead, it stresses the *existence* of genomes, and the *identification* of features, both of which are expressed passively. Phrases like "identification of features" and "genome-wide exploration" hide the active verbs "identify" and "explore" in strings of nouns and noun phrases; the second phrase is particularly confusing, because it doesn't say who's doing the exploring. Here's a less passive and more interesting version of the information:

> Understanding human evolution requires comparing genomes from related primates to the human genome. Fortunately, the past 5 years have seen several nonhuman primate genome sequences released that can help researchers identify which features are common among primates and which are unique to humans.

The point is that you can write well and still be scientific. The revised paragraph isn't full of slang and colloquialisms: it sounds empirical, cautious, and objective, yet it's perfectly understandable. That's the sort of tone you should aim for with most scientific writing.

1. https://cgi.duke.edu/web/sciwriting/index.php?action=lesson1

Appendix III

Audience and Tone

As with other college papers, your main audience for scientific papers will be your professor. But that doesn't mean that you should write only for her. You and your professor are together engaged in the polite fiction that your papers will be presented to a wider, more general scientific audience. (If they're really good, the fiction may become fact.) So it helps to envision readers who are educated and scientifically literate, but who may not know as much as you about the particular subject you've studied.

Because they're scientifically literate, your audience doesn't need basic concepts like *meiosis* and *mitosis* explained, but they will need specifics about your experiment or argument explained.

Science papers are usually more formal and objective in tone than those in some other college subjects (see Chapter 3), but that doesn't mean that they should be dense and stuffy. The fact that much scientific writing *is* dense and stuffy merely shows that scientific writers are getting bad advice about presenting their work. Editors of science journals today want better writing, and many encourage their writers to employ an active voice about people, things, and ideas. You can assume your audience won't be thrown for a loop by technical terms, but you'll still need to make sure that you present such terms clearly.

Telling a Story

Humanities papers are often about people, while science papers are often about things, but both benefit from the active voice—a *subject* doing something to an *object*. In practical terms, this means putting your verb as close as possible to your subject. In the case of the following weak sentence, the hidden verb is *to map* and the subject is the scientist doing the mapping, even though it's not stated in the sentence:

> Mapping of open chromatin regions, post-translational histone modifications and DNA methylation across a whole genome is now feasible, and new non-coding RNAs can be sensitively identified via RNA sequencing.[2]

By identifying who's doing what, and putting it near the verb, the sentence becomes much stronger:

---

2. https://cgi.duke.edu/web/sciwriting/index.php?action=lesson1

Scientists can now feasibly map open chromatin regions, post-translational histone modifications and DNA methylation across a whole genome, and sensitively identify new non-coding RNAs via RNA sequencing.

Anne Greene urges scientific writers to think of their subjects as "characters," even if they're not people: "By characters, I mean tangible, concrete nouns, like sandstone, aspen trees, or T cells," she writes. "The more concrete the characters and the more vigorous their actions, the better the story."

Her concept of scientific writing as *story* is worth keeping in mind. Since many papers review the work of other scientists, you can use references to those scientists as the subjects of your sentences. This example uses the active verb "showed" to tell a scientific story about *subjects* (Beyer et al.) who *showed* something about forest management and woodpeckers:

> Beyer et al. (1996) showed that many of the 0.8-km radius management circles around Red-cockaded Woodpecker groups in the Apalachicola National Forest are not in compliance with the current federal guidelines for minimum number of trees .25 cm dbh and total basal area in the foraging habitat.[3]

It's not exactly *Gone with the Wind*, but it's a story. Depending on your audience, you might need to explain the abbreviation *dbh* (diameter at breast height), along with the terms "management circles" and "total basal area." If, as this author is doing, you're writing for forestry biologists, who are familiar with such terms, that's probably not required.

Passive Voice and When to Use It

Chapter 6 explains how the active voice usually makes for better, clearer, and more concise sentences. But, particularly in scientific writing, you'll find many occasions when passive voice works best. For example, if you're writing a paper about carbohydrates, the following passive sentence works well:

> Carbohydrates are produced by green plants in the presence of light and chlorophyll.

If your paper were about the plants, however, active voice would be better:

> When light and chlorophyll are present, green plants produce carbohydrates.

---

3. Frances C. James, et al. "Ecosystem Management and the Niche Gestalt of the Red-Cockaded Woodpecker in Longleaf Pine Forests," *Ecological Applications* 11:3 (2001): 856.

Appendix III

When your sentence or paragraph focuses on *what is done* or *what is affected* rather than on who's doing it, passive voice is a good choice. This might be particularly important in the Methods section of a lab report or scientific paper. Passive voice also may make understanding easier in a paragraph where several sentences in a row have a consistent subject but different objects.

Word Choice

Don't inflate the diction of your sentences with unnecessarily complex words. Why use *implement* instead of *put into effect,* or *subsequent* instead of *next?* The classic example of this is employing *utilize* instead of *use* (or *eat,* or *drink*), which Ernest Hemingway memorably made fun of, describing two men getting drunk over dinner:

> "Let us utilize the fowls of the air. Let us utilize the product of the vine. Will you utilize a little, brother?"
> "After you, brother."
> Bill took a long drink.
> "Utilize a little, brother." He handed me the bottle.[4]

Besides inflated diction, another mark of weak scientific writing is overuse of noun strings. Noun strings are like freight trains of nouns, linked together and rattling down the track to form an impenetrable barrier for anyone seeking to cross into understanding.

Here's an example: "NASA continues to work on the *International Space Station astronaut living-quarters module development project.*" Why not call it a "project to develop the module for astronaut living quarters in the International Space Station"?

The U.S. government's "plain language" initiative gives the following phrase as an example of noun strings gone amok: "*Draft laboratory animal rights protection regulations.*" Instead, it says, try calling them "Draft regulations to protect the rights of laboratory animals."

In both examples above, the cure for long strings of nouns is putting them into sentences in which someone is doing something—*developing,* or *protecting*—with a strong verb and a clear subject.

Finally, look to cut out redundant words. The scientific journal publisher Elsevier cautions against phrases like "new result" and "latest finding" that

---

4. Ernest Hemingway, *The Sun Also Rises* (New York: Scribners, 2014), 96.

simply repeat themselves. And notice how many words are simply repeated or restated in the following paragraph, which Anne Greene gives as an example of wordiness:

> Despite the widely recognized importance of instream wood and organic debris dams in forested stream ecosystems, analytical approaches to quantify the spatial extent and pattern of instream wood distribution are rare and the usefulness of available metrics has been seldom evaluated. Wood influences stream geo-morphology, biotic habitat, and biogeochemical cycling, therefore quantifying the spatial distribution of instream wood is important for understanding the corresponding distribution of key stream functions.[5]

Techniques to Clarify Writing

Scientific papers are full of terminology that can become confusing, if you're not careful. A good writer essentially teaches his readers about the terminology as he writes it. One important way to do this is to present *old information* before *new information*. Consider the following paragraph:

> Populations of co-existing, closely related, but diverging variants of HCV RNA molecules are termed quasispecies. Quasispecies occur in many RNA viruses.[6]

Notice how the first sentence introduces information and gives it a name, *quasispecies*. Once that term is known to the reader, it becomes *old information*. Then the sentence moves on by repeating the old information and introducing *new information* about RNA viruses.

In the following paragraph, from the engineering department of the University of South Wales at Sidney, *old information* is printed in *italic type,* and **new information** is printed in **bold type**. Notice how it essentially teaches the reader new terms as it goes along:

> *Antibiotic resistant microorganisms* have significantly compromised **antibiotic treatment**. *A large proportion of resistance in Gram-negative bacteria* can be attributed to **resistance gene cassettes contained within a site-specific recombination system, termed the integron**. *Mobile cassettes* contain *genes* that **confer resistance to nearly every major class of antibiotic, and some disinfectants**. New *gene cassettes* continue to be identified and the *sequences of over 60 cassettes* are deposited in the **GenBank/EMBL databases**, as of January

---

5. Anne E. Greene, *Writing Science in Plain English* (Chicago: University of Chicago Press, 2013), 41.
6. https://student.unsw.edu.au/using-old-new-information-order-sentence

Appendix III

2001. This *rapid increase in the identification of gene cassettes* has led to the **same name being given to two different gene cassettes**, or the incorrect naming of gene cassettes. **This letter** aims to clarify the **current nomenclature for the aadA and dfr families of genes.**" (White 2007)[7]

Besides the old/new principle, the other important principle to remember in scientific writing is the one sketched out in Chapter 9—the principle of parallel structure. Instead of seeming repetitious, parallel structure actually makes your writing easier to understand. Think of numbered lists, where information is presented using a consistent format and structure:

1. Each piece of information gets its own number.
2. Each item uses a consistent grammatical structure.
3. Items build on those that come before them.
4. All items tend to be short and direct.

Presenting information in a parallel structure this way makes it more memorable and emphatic. But the principle of parallel structure isn't confined to lists.

Consider this paragraph from the journal *Protein Science*. Note the parallel elements that are *italicized*:

> *Symmetry of language is often helpful.* Parallel structures *within a sentence*, or *within adjacent sentences or paragraphs*, can often be used to good effect to hammer a point home. In this context, it *is more than acceptable* to repeat words or phrases in a sentence. ("While *it is largely accepted* that Chimps and Humans reside in *the same taxonomic order, there has been much debate* as to whether or not they reside in *the same taxonomic family*"). Conversely, *missed opportunities for symmetry* can create a void or hiccup in the text, as the reader's brain screeches to a halt after failing to find an anticipated parallel.[8]

Using parallel structure produces the subconscious effect of mapping out a route for information to follow, as rhyme does in a verse. You learn the route with the first parallel element, then you know to follow it in subsequent parallel elements. As a result, you can pay attention to the new items that are introduced rather than having to pause and figure out whether you've already learned something in an earlier phrase or sentence.

Finally, clear scientific writing tends to progress from the general to the specific, as in this example from the University of Maryland:

---

7. https://student.unsw.edu.au/using-old-new-information-order-sentence
8. Kevin W. Plaxco, "The Art of Writing Science," *Protein Science* 19: 12 (2010): par. 12. https://www.ncbi.nlm.nih.gov/pmc/articles/PMC3009394/.

Writing in the Sciences

Writing is a complex sociocognitive process involving the construction of recorded messages on paper or on some other material, and, more recently, on a computer screen. The skills needed to write range from making the appropriate graphic marks, through utilizing the resources of the chosen language, to anticipating the reactions of the intended readers. The first skill area involves acquiring a writing system, which may be alphabetic (as in European languages) or nonalphabetic (as in many Asian languages). The second skill area requires selecting the appropriate grammar and vocabulary to form acceptable sentences and then arranging them in paragraphs. Third, writing involves thinking about the purpose of the text to be composed and about its possible effects on the intended readership. One important aspect of this last feature is the choice of a suitable style. Because of these characteristics, writing is not an innate natural ability like speaking but has to be acquired through years of training or schooling (Swales & Feak, 1994, p. 34).[9]

Notice how the paragraph above begins with something general—the process of writing—and moves to more and more specific information about that process. Once again, the idea is to teach the reader as you go, providing information that builds on what has come before. In scientific writing, this is particularly important, as the results of a scientific experiment or study develop out of the background and procedures of the experiment or study.

The main thing to remember about scientific writing in college is that although the information is often quite specialized and of interest to a very limited audience, that audience is human. Human beings of all sorts struggle with unclear writing, and anything that you can do to make their work easier will get your work more attention, respect, and, if the science behind it is good too, better grades.

---

9. https://coursedev.umuc.edu/WRTG999A/chapter3/ch3-10.html

Index

abstraction 28, 29, 30, 31, 32, 62, 74, 79, 151; high-level 28; trap of 31
abstractions 26
academic argumentation 19
academic conversation 106, 146
academic journals 145; writing for 7
academic writing: as science 25
action 34
active verbs 15, 16, 18, 171
active voice 33, 34, 35, 36, 54, 172, 173
Ad Baculum fallacy 71, 156
Ad Hominem fallacy 71, 155
Ad Ignorantiam fallacy 71, 156
Ad Misericordiam fallacy 71, 156
Ad Populum fallacy 71, 156
Ad Vericundiam fallacy 71, 155
aesthetics 12
Affirming the Consequent fallacy 157
agency statement *see* agent
agent 35, 103, 106, 108, 113, 114, 115, 116, 117, 118, 119, 120, 122, 132, 133, 143, 151, 153
Alexa 105
Alice's Adventures in Wonderland 108
The Amazing Spider-Man 118
American Psychological Association 164
analogy 110
analogy or parallel case: introduction strategy 110
analysis 19, 60, 61, 63, 64, 90, 129, 151, 152, 170
analytical paragraphs 61, 63
argued/argues 90
argument 5, 21, 23, 25, 45, 46, 47, 48, 49, 50, 55, 57, 58, 59, 60, 62, 63, 64, 65, 66, 68, 70, 72, 88, 89, 103, 104, 106, 107, 108, 116, 117, 121, 122, 126, 133, 137, 147, 155, 172; spoken aloud 64
argumentation: compared to persuasion 47; contemporary model for 66; essay plan 122, 133
Aristotle 50, 70, 120, 122, 126
art 18; meaning 11
arts: fine 11
Arts and Sciences: colleges of 10
Associated Press Stylebook 161
attributive verbs 90

audience 1, 6, 7, 8, 13, 15, 25, 29, 30, 37, 38, 39, 58, 66, 68, 93, 98, 101, 103, 106, 107, 113, 116, 117, 118, 121, 138, 148, 150, 151, 175, 177, 178
Austen, Jane 107
avoiding plagiarism 94

background information 89
backing 58, 59, 60
bad data 67, 68
bandwidth 5, 30
BASIC 12
Basic Analytical Paragraph 61, 125
Beale, Walter 105, 107, 109
Begging the Question fallacy 71, 156
Berke, Jacqueline 79
Beyoncé 106
Biased Statistics fallacy 158
bibliographic entry 93
biology 24
Blackburn, Paul 22, 23
blogs 81; to generate ideas 81
body: of essay 119
books: print 87
Boolean search terms 86
botany 31
Brady, Tom 59
brainstorming 74, 77, 78, 81, 105
B.S. 2, 13, 67, 68, 69, 152
Buber, Martin 18
Bulwer-Lytton, Lord 30
Bush, George W. 48, 49 131, 159
Butler, Samuel 138

C++ 12
California 55
Carroll, Lewis 33, 35, 108
case studies 12
causal chain 131
cause: immediate 131; primary 131; remote 131; secondary 131
cause and effect 130, 136; essay plan 121, 130
Chaplain, Charlie 55
character: in argument 46
characters 36, 171, 173
Chicago Manual of Style 167

Index

Chicago style 92, 162, 167, 168, 175
Chinese language 11
Cicero 64, 66
Ciceronian argumentation 64
Circular Reasoning fallacy 156
citations 25
Citizen Kane 57
claims 23, 45, 49, 52, 53, 54, 57, 58, 59, 60, 61, 64, 65, 66, 67, 70, 89, 90, 114, 132, 151, 155; of fact 57; of interpretation 57; of policy 57; truth of 58; of value 57
clarity 26
Classical Argumentation 64, 133
Classical Model for Argumentation 64
classics 24
classification 132, 136
clauses: nonrestrictive 12; restrictive 12
clichés 6, 52, 111, 150; academic 45
closure 139
Cobb, Lee J. 44
cognitive psychology 11, 30
Colbert, Stephen 55
college: purpose 6
college degree 35
college papers: tone 7
college writing 29; objectivity 19
colon: use in titles 147, 149
color theory 11
common knowledge 52, 55, 56
common sense 13, 46, 69
communication 4, 5, 6, 28, 30, 62, 132, 170
comparison: essay plan 121, 126; of parts 127; point-to-point 126; of similarities and differences 126; subject-to-subject 126; of wholes 127
comparison and contrast 120, 126, 136
Complex Question fallacy 71, 157
complimentary closings 8
composition fallacies 157
comprehensiveness 26
computer models 11
concession 65, 151
conclusion 19, 38, 40, 46, 54, 65, 66, 68, 96, 100, 101, 104, 108, 112, 114, 116, 117, 119, 133, 138, 139, 140, 142, 143, 144, 158; analogy or parallel case 141; answer to question 140; answering "who cares?" and "so what?" 142; compelling quote 140; confession or personal note 141; link to opening 142; provocative afterthought 139; question to ponder 140; rebuttal 141; redefining key term 142; thesis 139; thesis implications 142
concrete and specific writing 74
conditions: necessary 131
confession or personal introduction: introduction strategy 111
confirmatio 65
confirmation 66

contemporary model for argumentation 65
Cooley, Mason 1
copular construction 12
correspondence 8
Council of Science Editors 166
court: as deliberative model 45
creative writing 19
critical lens 96, 97
critical thinking 4, 7, 35, 63, 126
CSE style 92, 162, 166
curriculum: arts and sciences 11

data 5, 8, 13, 17, 20, 22, 23, 24, 25, 29, 31, 50, 52, 55, 61, 62, 63, 64, 65, 66, 67, 68, 69, 82, 88, 89, 91, 124, 125, 151, 152, 154, 170; and academic writing 22; "cherry-picking" 69; misuse of 25; as singular and plural 22
databases: searching 1, 86, 87, 163, 164, 175
dates and common knowledge 55
Dawkins, Richard 104
deadlines 80
deduction: logical 70
definition 134, 142; dictionary 134; essay plan 122, 133; extended 135; formal 135; negative 134; stipulated 136
definitions and common knowledge 55
deliberation 65; academic 45
Denying the Antecedent fallacy 71, 157
Denying the Consequent fallacy 71
derivations: and common knowledge 55
Derrida, Jacques 83
description 19, 29, 110, 120, 123, 124, 136
description/narration: essay plan 121
details 23, 26, 32, 55, 74, 75, 78, 79, 124, 125; sensory 29; specific 1, 26
Dickinson, Emily 119
dictionary 134
discipline 98
disciplines: academic 24
distribution fallacies 71, 157
division 132
division and classification: essay plan 121, 132
division fallacies 157
Dobson, James 97
documentation 91
"documentation sandwich" 93
Donne, John 162
drafts: writing in 4, 74, 80, 130, 150
Drum, Kevin 109

economics 24
editorial voice: and brainstorming 78
Einstein, Albert 74
Eliot, T.S. 26, 150
email 8, 76
Emancipation Proclamation 121
emotions: in argument 47
emphasis 40, 138; first and last positions 40

180

Index

endnotes 163
English: colloquial 7; language 14
epistemology: and college writing 52, 53
Equivocation fallacy 71, 157
essay exam 12, 112, 113, 117, 120, 126
essay structure 102
essays 4, 5, 7, 52, 54, 61, 63, 65, 66, 68, 79, 89, 91, 100, 101, 102, 103, 104, 106, 107, 109, 112, 113, 114, 115, 116, 117, 118, 119, 121, 123, 126, 134, 135, 136, 137, 145, 148; personal 24
ethos 46, 47
evidence 7, 9, 21, 23, 45, 46, 47, 53, 61, 67, 115, 136, 144, 158
examples 30, 49, 52, 55, 61, 66, 71, 86, 96, 100, 115, 120, 124, 127, 132, 135, 146, 174
exams 4; studying for 5
exordium 64
expert opinion 89
expertise 88; fake 13
experts: writing for 7
expletive construction 12
expository writing 19

fact checkers 24
facts 6, 7, 8, 13, 18, 23, 24, 34, 44, 45, 47, 48, 49, 52, 55, 58, 65, 66, 68, 70, 80, 82, 88, 92, 98, 117, 119, 124, 152, 154
factual accuracy 60
fallacies 70, 71, 72, 155, 158
fallacy: logical 70, 155, 157, 158, 159
Fallacy of Biased Statistics 71
Fallacy of Insufficient Statistics 71
Fallacy of Many Questions 157
False Analogy fallacy 71, 158
False Precedent fallacy 71
Fears, J. Rufus 110
feels/believes 91
fiction 4
first draft 6, 80
first person 7
first-year writing 52, 146
five-paragraph essay 66
Focus on the Family 97
focusing event: introduction strategy 110
focusing question: introduction strategy 110
focusing quotation: introduction strategy 110
Fonda, Henry 44
footnotes 4, 8, 25, 92, 93, 95, 154, 161, 163, 164, 166, 167, 168
Fox News 68
Frankfurt, Harry G. 61, 63
freewriting 78
full-text databases 87
fun 153

The Gambler's Fallacy 72, 160
generalities 30
generalizing 27

geography: and common knowledge 55
gerunds 18
Gettysburg Address 38, 39
Gone with the Wind 173
Google 6, 82, 83, 84, 85, 86
Gopen, George 170
Gore, Al 48, 49, 131
grammar 12, 17, 30, 78, 91, 150, 178; of quotations 25; rules of 12
Greene, Anne E. 171, 173, 175
Guilt by Association fallacy 71, 158
Gusoff, Adrienne 112

Hand, Learned 22
harmonics 11
Harris, Sam 57
Hasty Generalization fallacy 71, 158
Hemingway, Ernest 174
Henry, Patrick 55
high-quality information: finding 84
high school: writing in 7, 8, 29, 51, 56, 66, 100, 101, 105
Hitchens, Christopher 64
honesty: academic 8
house of ideas 102, 113, 151

"I feel" 9
"I think" 9
imagination 74, 77, 78, 139, 151
index cards 77
Indus Valley Language 27
information 88; sorting out 83
Insufficient Statistics fallacy 158
intelligent discourse 6, 7
Inter-library loan 85
Internet: reliability of information on 83
interpretation 104
interpreter 27
introductions 1, 40, 66, 96, 97, 105, 106, 107, 108, 109, 112, 113, 114, 115, 133, 140, 143, 148, 151; ineffective 111
inverted pyramid 106
Irrelevant Conclusion fallacy 71, 158

Jackson, Brooks 48
Jamestown 68
Jamieson, Kathleen Hall 48
jargon 31
journalism 19, 105
journals 74, 81, 174, 177; scholarly 7
Joyce, James 30

Kandinsky, Wassily 78
Kardashian, Kim 106
Kaufman, Charlie 145
keywords 85, 86, 148
King, Martin Luther, Jr. 55, 115, 116
Kipling, Rudyard 88

181

Index

Kirkegaard, Søren 17
Kneiger, Bernard 89
knowledge 9

La-La Land 57
lab reports 5, 129
Lamott, Anne: *Bird by Bird* 80
language 5, 6, 7, 15, 27, 28, 30, 31, 39, 62, 83, 89, 94, 95, 115, 130, 174, 177, 178; colloquial 31
Lanham, Richard 13, 15, 153; Paramedic Method of revision 15
Latin 31
Lawrence, D.H. 100
Leckie, Ann 161
lectures 4
lede 106
Leibniz, Gottfried 61
letter: job application 8
letters 4
librarians 84, 85, 87; contact by text message 85; contacting 85; expertise of 85
library catalog 87
Library of Congress Subject Headings 87
library resources 85
lies 5, 47, 68, 69, 71
Lincoln, Abraham 38, 39, 121
linguistics 11, 12
Linguistics Journal 83
LISP 12
lists: and the Objective Style 14; and parallel structure 40, 41
literature 88
logic 12, 19, 26, 46, 47, 49, 52, 59, 60, 67, 69, 70, 71, 72, 101, 116, 119, 132, 151, 155, 156; faulty 67

manners: writing as etiquette 12
A Manual for Writers of Research Papers, Theses, and Dissertations 168
mapping: brainstorming technique 79
mathematics 24
Mayflower Pilgrims 68
meme 104
memos 4
meteorology 29
Mexico 55
Mizner, Wilson 10
Modern Language Association 163
modifiers: misplaced 12
Morin, Richard 110

Nagumo, Adm. Chuichi 56
names: and common knowledge 55
narratio 65
narration 66
narration and description: essay plan 123, 125
narrative 123, 124, 125, 127

Narrow Sampling fallacy 71, 158
new information 175
New York Times 83
Nietzsche, Friedrich 24
Non Sequitur fallacy 157
note-taking 5, 7, 12, 74, 75, 81; map style 74; and plagiarism 94; recording lectures 77; summary style 74; verbatim style 74
noun phrases 18, 171
noun strings 174
nouns 18

object 17
Objective Style 13, 14, 15, 17, 18, 20, 30, 33, 35, 36, 67, 96, 152, 153, 170
objectivity 18, 19, 20, 21, 23, 170; academic 17
Odysseus 47, 48
old information 175
open house: model for essays 102, 103, 113, 119
opinions: reasoned 7; uninformed 9
organization 1
Orwell, George 62, 115; "Politics and the English Language" 132
Oxford English Dictionary 10

paper: college 6, 59, 65, 66, 105
paper assignments: rationale for 4
paragraph 5, 79
parallel structure 39, 40, 128, 177
parallelism 39, 40
Paramedic Method: technique for revision 15, 18, 33, 153
paraphrasing 34, 63, 89, 94; and plagiarism 94; use of 25
parenthetical references 92, 163
participles: dangling 12
partitio 65
passive voice 12, 33, 35, 36, 173, 174; uses of 35
pathos 46, 47
PDF format 86
Pearl Harbor 56
peer-reviewed journals 84
peroratio 65
personal experience 52, 59, 107, 141
persuasion 47, 48, 49, 70, 71, 155, 156
Pinker, Stephen 30
plagiarism 25, 92, 94, 95; punishment 25
plain language 16
plan 48, 102, 103, 104, 108, 119, 120, 122, 126, 129, 151, 152
Plato 50, 120, 122, 126
Plymouth Rock 68
poetry 4, 20, 23, 24, 26, 29, 82, 91, 139
point of view: objective 17; subjective 18
popular culture 1
Portable Document Format (PDF) 86
Post Hoc Fallacy 72, 159
premises 67

182

Index

prepositional phrases: overuse of 14, 15, 16, 36
problem or controversy: introduction strategy 109
process 136
process analysis 129
process analysis and explanation: essay plan 121, 128
process explanation 129
proof 49
psychology 12, 70, 86, 162
punctuation 8, 37, 162, 163, 165, 166

quantum mechanics 11
Queen Elizabeth II 55
Queensbury, Marquis of 49
quotation: use of 25, 88
quotation and paraphrase: mixing 95
quotation marks: in note-taking 76
quotations: accuracy of 24; and common knowledge 55; in MLA style 163; overuse of 90

reader *see* audience
reasoning 9
reasons 8, 52, 65, 66, 115, 151
rebuttal: introduction strategy 109
Red Herring fallacy 72, 159
referent 27
refutation 60, 65, 66, 96, 133, 151
Reid, Harry 68
reports 4
reproducible results 91
research 13, 15, 19, 45, 47, 52, 55, 59, 66, 73, 86, 88, 89, 95, 96, 97, 98, 105, 108, 110, 119, 130, 143, 145, 149, 151
revision 6, 150; comparing 6; empathizing 6; ruminating 6
rhetorical question 140
rhythm: prose 35; in writing 37, 38, 40, 41, 153
Rogerian argument 133
Rogers, Carl 133
Rose, Reginald 44

said 34
said/says 90
salutations 8
Santayana, George 4
Santiago de Compostela 86
scholar: role of 82
scholarly journals 50
science: academic writing as 9, 10; in college argument 47; fake 13, 14, 30; meaning of 11; writing as 12
sciences: hard 11; writing in the 170–178
scientific method 17
scientific writing 22, 35, 170, 171, 172, 173, 174, 177, 178
scientist: writer as 63

scientists 13, 69, 109, 170, 171, 173
self-censoring 80
semiotic theory 27
semiotic triangle 27
Sense and Sensibility 107
sentences 5, 7; diagramming 12; fragments 7; ungrammatical 7
"sex objects" 17
Shakespeare, William 11
shorthand 75
"Show, don't tell" 29
"shuffle" notes 77
sign 27, 28
sign vehicle 27
Siri 105
skepticism 1, 7, 52, 54, 60, 65, 68, 69, 151, 153
slang 7
Slippery Slope Fallacy 72, 159
smartphone 5, 77, 82, 83
smell 27
"so what?" question 8, 16, 54, 60, 132, 143, 146, 147
Socrates 44
sound 27
sources: documentation of 24
specific and concrete 79
specific versus general 27
specificity 29
specifics 30, 31, 32
spelling 8, 78, 150
standards 1
states 34
statisticians 69
statistics 22, 23, 24, 66, 69, 83; use of 25
Stengel, Casey 82
stories 123
Straw Man fallacy 72, 159
stream of consciousness 30
structure: in writing 38
Strunk, William, Jr. 37, 39
style 12; APA 4, 25, 92, 162, 164, 165; MLA 4, 24, 92, 162, 163; rules of 8; scientific 13
style guides 161
subject 17
subjectivity 13, 18, 19, 20, 23, 29, 170; and objectivity 20
subtitles 147, 149
summary 5, 25, 95, 124
supporting information 58, 59, 96
Swann, Judith 170
synthesis: compared to analysis 129

takeaway 104, 116, 118, 132, 133, 138, 139, 143, 144, 148, 151
taste 11, 27
term paper 5
terminology 151
testimony 24, 45, 66, 88, 89

183

Index

texting 8
theory 98
thesis 54, 57, 59, 65, 66, 96, 97, 100, 101, 103, 104, 105, 106, 108, 109, 110, 112, 113, 114, 115, 116, 117, 132, 138, 139, 140, 143, 148, 151
thesis opening: introduction strategy 109
Thomas, Dylan 89, 93
Thoreau, Henry David 115, 116
three-legged stool: argument as 46
threshold 102, 103, 106, 107, 111, 112, 113, 116, 117, 118, 119, 133, 151
title: and reader comprehension 145
titles 145, 147, 149; composing 145; qualities of good 146
"To be": overuse of 14, 15, 16, 18
tone: academic 7; informal 7; personal 8; scholarly subjects 7; scientific 7, 13
topic: paper 5
topic sentence 112
touch 27
Toulmein, Stephen 58; theory of argument 58
transitional and connecting words 152
transitions 152
Trump, Donald 57, 70, 139
truncation characters: and searches 87
truth 49
Tu Quoque fallacy 72, 155
Turabian, Kate L. 168
Turabian Style 162
Twain, Mark 23
12 Angry Men, 44
twenty questions: brainstorming technique 79; two-minute summaries 76; Two Wrongs fallacy 72, 159

Unamuno, Miguel de 51
University of Chicago Press 167
usage 12

vagueness 27
verbals 18
verbs: active 16, 33, 173
visual thinker 75

Wallace, David Foster 54
warrant 58, 59, 60, 151
White, E.B. 142
"who says?" question 52, 53, 60
Wi-Fi 82
Wikipedia 83, 84, 130, 132; problems with using 84
Williams, Serena 55
Williams, William Carlos 26
Wired Magazine 83
wit 153
The Wizard of Oz 14
word snapshots: brainstorming technique 79
works cited 93; list of 163
Wright Brothers 52
writing: academic 1, 9, 22, 24, 25, 36, 45, 53, 55, 67, 91, 161; bad 1, 6, 12; boring 17; clear 26; college 1, 4, 10, 18, 19, 20, 23, 24, 28, 29, 33, 35, 36, 45, 47, 50, 53, 61, 67, 68, 69, 81, 100, 121, 161; comprehensive 27; formal 5; good 1, 12, 39, 40, 74, 150, 170; to learn 5; learning by doing 12; learning by reading 12; for others 4, 5, 6, 32; scientific 13, 35; for yourself 4, 5, 7, 32
Writing Science in Plain English 171
wrote/writes 90

www.ingramcontent.com/pod-product-compliance
Ingram Content Group UK Ltd.
Pitfield, Milton Keynes, MK11 3LW, UK
UKHW042013140426
5217IPUK00015B/1157